W9-CBB-285

PRAYERS THAT AVAIL MUCH®

VOLUME 1

James 5:16

by
Germaine Copeland

And this is the confidence that we have in him, that, if we ask any thing according to his will, he heareth us: and if we know that he hear us, whatsoever we ask, we know that we have the petitions that we desired of him.

1 John 5:14,15

Harrison House
Tulsa, Oklahoma

Unless otherwise indicated, all Scripture quotations are taken from the *King James Version* of the Bible.

Scripture quotations marked AMP are taken from *The Amplified Bible, Old Testament,* copyright © 1965, 1987 by the Zondervan Corporation. *The Amplified Bible, New Testament,* copyright © 1958, 1987 by the Lockman Foundation. Used by permission.

Prayers and confessions are paraphrased from these verses unless otherwise stated.

Prayers That Avail Much is a registered trademark of Word Ministries, Inc., a Georgia corporation.

3rd Printing

Prayers That Avail Much®, *Volume 1* —
ISBN 1-57794-282-5
(Formerly ISBN 0-89274-590-8)
Copyright © 1999 by Germaine Copeland

Germaine Copeland
President, Word Ministries, Inc.
38 Sloan St.
Roswell, Georgia 30075

Published by Harrison House, Inc.
P. O. Box 35035
Tulsa, Oklahoma 74153

Printed in the United States of America. All rights reserved under International Copyright Law. Contents and/or cover may not be reproduced in whole or in part in any form without the express written consent of the Publisher.

Dedication

This book is dedicated to our Lord and Savior, Jesus Christ.

**The Lord gave the Word: great was
the company of those that published it.
Psalm 68:11**

Special thanks to Jan Duncan, Carolyn East, Pat Gastineau, Frankie Patterson, Barbara Patton and Pat Porter for their share in this book.

Germaine Copeland, President
Word Ministries, Inc.

Contents

The Genesis of Prayers That Avail Much   7
Foreword   12
Introduction   17
Personal Confessions   31
Prayers of Praise   34

I.   Personal Prayers

Prayers of Commitment

1	To Walk in the Word	41
2	To Be God-Inside Minded	44
3	To Rejoice in the Lord	47
4	To Walk in God's Wisdom and His Perfect Will	50
5	To Walk in Love	53
6	To Walk in Forgiveness	56
7	To Watch What You Say	58
8	To Live Free From Worry	60
9	To Receive Jesus As Savior and Lord	63
10	To Receive the Infilling of the Holy Spirit	65

Prayers for Personal Concerns

11	Boldness	69
12	Husbands	72
13	Wives	74
14	Harmonious Marriage	77
15	Compatibility in Marriage	79
16	The Children	82
17	The Home	85
18	Prosperity	87
19	Dedication for Your Tithes	89
20	Health and Healing	91
21	Safety	93
22	Victory Over Fear	95

23	Victory Over Depression	97
24	Victory in a Healthy Lifestyle	100
25	In Court Cases	102

II. Intercessory Prayers for Others

Prayers for God's People and Ministries

26	The Body of Christ	109
27	Ministers	112
28	Missionaries	115
29	Prosperity for Ministering Servants	119
30	Success of a Meeting	123

Prayers for the World

31	Salvation of the Lost	129
32	Nations and Continents	131
33	Peace of Jerusalem	140

Prayers for Those in Authority

34	American Government	145
35	School Systems and Children	148

Prayers for the Needs of Others

36	Salvation	155
37	Spirit-Controlled Life	157
38	Renew Fellowship	160
39	Deliverance From Satan and His Demonic Forces	163
40	Employment	168
41	Finding Favor With Others	171
42	Improving Communication	174
43	Peace in a Troubled Marriage	177
44	Single Believer	179
45	Single Female Trusting God for a Mate	181
46	Single Male Trusting God for a Mate	183
47	Prayer for Those With Special Needs	185
48	Deliverance From Corrupt Companions	188
49	Deliverance From Cults	191
50	Deliverance From Habits	196

The Prayers of Jesus	201
The Prayers of Paul	209

The Genesis of Prayers
That Avail Much

*T*his handbook of scriptural prayers was written for you. We at Word Ministries believe that this volume will help you to know how to pray in given situations and will strengthen your faith in God.

I first began writing prayers as a result of studying the Scriptures and reading materials written by experienced praying Christians. It was an in-depth study of 1 John 5:14-15 that revolutionized my prayer life. I had been fellowshipping with the Father, Son and Holy Spirit, using certain Psalms as an expression of praise and worship. Now began a new adventure for me—presenting my petitions before the throne of grace according to the promises of God.

Our Father declared that His Word would not return to Him void or without accomplishing His purpose. Since many authors over the past centuries recorded His Words through the inspiration of the Holy Spirit, I believed that I could agree with Him by personalizing the Scriptures. My confidence that He would hear me grew, and I began to pray for my family, church and friends with fervency.

On an eventful day in the life of my family, I recognized that the enemy had launched an attack on our home, hurling us into a crisis that would consume and confound us for many years. The situation was beyond our control, and I wanted above all else to know how to pray effectively. I sought the Lord, and He heard me.

I was in church on a Sunday morning sitting next to a friend when I received my commission to pen my prayer requests as confessions of faith. While pointing to her Bible, she leaned toward me, whispering, "While I was praying for you today, the Lord gave me this Scripture." It was Isaiah 54:13. She didn't know about the adverse circumstances in our home, but the Holy Spirit did. This verse from the *King James Version* was the basis for the very first prayer I wrote. **And all thy children shall be taught of the Lord; and great shall be the peace of thy children** (Isa. 54:13).

After meditating on this verse in various translations, I finally chose *The Amplified Bible* as my prayer book. I added more and more Scriptures to the prayer, and as time went on I shared this written prayer with other parents.

After I organized an intercessory prayer group, using God's Word as our foundation, others began writing prayers. One group member, Carolyn East of Atlanta, became our "intercessory prayer journalist." We scanned our concordances and Bibles for Scriptures pertaining to the various prayer requests that we were receiving from people all over the Atlanta area. Carolyn diligently wrote the Scriptures in prayer form and distributed them for us. She attended the Bible study which I was teaching and did research, pursuing ministers and their prayer coordinators for answers to questions with which we were struggling. Carolyn also typed the foreword and introduction from materials taught in my Bible class lessons.

We wrote prayers and also collected them from other sources. This book did not materialize overnight. There were many stages. Hand-printed ditto sheets of paper graduated to a typed, hand-stapled form. At one time we enlisted the help of a vocational workshop program director, whose students printed and bound the prayers in spiral, cookbook fashion. To this day we receive calls from people who want to order this informal edition.

Carolyn East and Jan Duncan, who typed the final manuscript and opened her home for our work center, had the vision for worldwide distribution. We agreed that this labor of love would cover the world, delivering souls and transforming lives. We prayed, and God provided the funds.

We contacted ministers whom we considered to be excellent teachers, sending them copies of our unpretentious publication. We requested and received permission to use their books, prayers and/or audio-tapes as references. We approached publishers with the manuscript, and it was Harrison House who agreed to publish our book, contingent upon our furnishing the cost of the first publication.

Now you hold the assemblage of the prayers of personal concerns written by others, and prayers of confessions that I wrote for myself, my husband, my children and others who requested prayer. Today your prayer requests are prayed for in this same manner. We continue to write prayers, sending them to many of those for whom we pray.

I am so blessed when I reread those first prayers and realize that God has proven Himself faithful again and again to watch over His Word to perform it. I am encouraged to continue in faith, believing God for those yet unanswered prayers. God does not always work according to our time schedules, but He does hear and answer prayer. Confess these prayers for yourself and on behalf of others.

But thanks be to God, Who gives us the victory [making us conquerors] through our Lord Jesus Christ. Therefore, my beloved brethren, be firm (steadfast), immovable, always abounding in the work of the Lord [always being superior, excelling, doing more than enough in the service of the Lord], knowing and being continually aware that your labor in the Lord is not futile [it is never wasted or to no purpose].

1 Corinthians 15:57,58 AMP

— Germaine Copeland
President, Word Ministries, Inc.

How to Pray
Prayers That Avail Much®

*T*he prayers in this book are to be used by you for yourself and for others. They are a matter of the heart. Deliberately pray and meditate on each prayer. Allow the Holy Spirit to make the Word a reality in your heart. Your spirit will become alive to God's Word, and you will begin to think like God thinks and talk like He talks. You will find yourself poring over His Word, hungering for more and more. The Father rewards those who diligently seek Him. (Heb. 11:6.)

Research and contemplate the spiritual significance of each verse listed with the prayers. These are by no means the only Scriptures on certain subjects, but they are a beginning.

These prayers are a guide for you to have a more intimate relationship with your heavenly Father. The study of his Word transforms your mind and lifestyle. Then, others will know that it is possible to change, and you will give hope to those who come to you seeking advice. When you admonish someone with the Word, you are offering spiritual guidance and consolation.

Walk in God's counsel, and prize His wisdom. (Ps. 1; Prov. 4:7,8.) People are looking for something on which they can depend. When someone in need comes to you, you can point him to that portion in God's Word that is the answer to his problem. You become victorious, trustworthy, and the one with the answer, for your heart is fixed and established on His Word. (Ps. 112.)

Once you begin delving into God's Word, you must commit to ordering your conversation aright. (Ps. 50:23.) That is being a doer of the Word. Faith always has a good report. You cannot pray effectively for yourself, for someone else or about something and then talk negatively about the matter. (Matt. 12:34-37.) This is being double-minded, and a double-minded man receives *nothing* from God. (James 1:6-8.)

In Ephesians 4:29-30 AMP it is written:

Let no foul or polluting language, nor evil word, nor unwholesome or worthless talk [ever] come out of your mouth;

but only such [speech] as is good and beneficial to the spiritual progress of others, as is fitting to the need and the occasion, that it may be a blessing and give grace (God's favor) to those who hear it.

And do not grieve the Holy Spirit of God, (do not offend, or vex, or sadden Him) by whom you were sealed (marked, branded as God's own, secured) for the day of redemption—of final deliverance through Christ from evil and the consequences of sin.

Reflect on these words and give them time to keep your perspective in line with God's will. Our Father has much, so very much, to say about that little member, the tongue. (James 3.) Give the devil no opportunity by getting into worry, unforgiveness, strife and criticism. Put a stop to idle and foolish talking. (Eph. 4:27; 5:4.) You are to be a blessing to others. (Gal. 6:10.)

Talk the answer, not the problem. The answer is in God's Word. You must have knowledge of that Word— revelation knowledge. (1 Cor. 2:7-16.) The Holy

Spirit, your teacher, will reveal the things that have been freely give to us by God. (John 14:26.)

As an intercessor, unite with others in prayer. United prayer is a mighty weapon that the Body of Christ is to use.

Have the faith of God, and approach Him confidently. When you pray according to His will, He hears you. Then you know you have what you ask of Him. (I John 5:14-15 NIV.) Do not throw away your confidence. It will be richly rewarded. (Hebrews 10:35 NIV.) Allow your spirit to pray by the Holy Spirit. Praise God for the victory now before any manifestation. *Walk by faith and not by sight.* (2 Cor. 5:7.)

When your faith comes under pressure, don't be moved. As Satan attempts to challenge you, resist him steadfast in the faith—letting patience have her perfect work. (James 1:4.) Take the Sword of the Spirit and the shield of faith and quench his every fiery dart. (Eph. 6:16,17.) The entire substitutionary work of Christ was for you. Satan is now a defeated foe because Jesus conquered him. (Col. 2:14,15.) Satan is overcome by the blood of the Lamb and the word of our testimony. (Rev. 12:11.) Fight the good fight of faith. (1 Tim. 6:12.) Withstand the adversary and be firm in faith against his onset—rooted, established, strong and determined. (1 Pet. 5:9.) Speak God's Word boldly and courageously.

Your desire should be to please and to bless the Father. As you pray according to His Word, He joyfully hears that you—His child—are living and walking in the Truth. (3 John 4.)

How exciting to know that the prayers of the saints are forever in the throne room. (Rev. 5:8.) Hallelujah!

Praise God for His Word and the limitlessness of prayer in the name of Jesus. It belongs to every child of God. Therefore, run with patience the race that is set before you, looking unto Jesus, the author and finisher of your faith. (Heb. 12:1,2.) God's Word is able to build you up and give you your rightful inheritance among all God's set apart ones. (Acts 20:32.)

Commit yourself to pray and to pray correctly by approaching the throne with your mouth filled with His Word!

Effectual Prayer

*T*he earnest (heart-felt, continued) prayer of a righteous man makes tremendous power available—dynamic in its working.

James 5:16 AMP

Prayer is fellowshipping with the Father—a vital, personal contact with God, Who is more than enough. We are to be in constant communion with Him:

For the eyes of the Lord are upon the righteous—those who are upright and in right standing with God—and His ears are attentive (open) to their prayer....

1 Peter 3:12 AMP

Prayer is not to be a religious form with no power. It is to be effective and accurate and bring *results*. God watches over His Word to perform it. (Jer. 1:12.)

Prayer that brings results must be based on God's Word.

> For the Word that God speaks is
> alive and full of power—making it
> active, operative, energizing and effec-
> tive; it is sharper than any two-edged
> sword, penetrating to the dividing line
> of the breath of life (soul) and [the
> immortal] spirit, and of joints and
> marrow [that is, of the deepest parts of
> our nature] exposing and sifting and
> analyzing and judging the very thoughts
> and purposes of the heart.
>
> Hebrews 4:12 AMP

Prayer is this "living" Word in our mouths. Our mouths must speak forth faith, for faith is what pleases God. (Heb. 11:6.) We hold His Word up to Him in prayer, and our Father sees Himself in His Word.

God's Word is our contact with Him. We put Him in remembrance of His Word (Is. 43:26), asking Him for what we need in the name of our Lord Jesus. The woman in Mark 5:25-34 placed a demand on the power of God when she said, "If I can but touch the hem of his garment I will be healed." By faith she touched his clothes and was healed. We remind Him that He supplies all of our needs according to His riches in glory by Christ Jesus. (Phil. 4:19.) That Word does not return to Him void—without producing any effect, useless—but it *shall* accomplish that which He pleases and purposes, and it shall prosper in the thing for which He sent it. (Isa. 55:11.) Hallelujah!

God did *not* leave us without His thoughts and His ways, for we have His Word—His bond. God instructs us to call Him, and He will answer and show us great and mighty things. (Jer. 33:3.) Prayer is to be exciting—not drudgery.

It takes someone to pray. God moves as we pray in faith—believing. He says that His eyes run to and fro throughout the whole earth to show Himself strong in behalf of those whose hearts are blameless toward Him. (2 Chron. 16:9.) We are blameless. (Eph. 1:4.) We are His very own children. (Eph. 1:5.) We are His righteousness in Christ Jesus. (2 Cor. 5:21.) He tells us to come boldly to the throne of grace and *obtain* mercy and find grace to help in time of need—appropriate and well-timed help. (Heb. 4:16.) Praise the Lord!

The prayer armor is for every believer, every member of the Body of Christ, who will put it on and walk in it, for the weapons of our warfare are *not carnal* but mighty through God for the pulling down of the strongholds of the enemy (Satan, the god of this world, and all his demonic forces). Spiritual warfare takes place in prayer. (2 Cor. 10:4; Eph. 6:12,18.)

There are many different kinds of prayer, such as the prayer of thanksgiving and praise, the prayer of dedication and worship and the prayer that changes things (not God). All prayer involves a time of fellow-shipping with the Father.

In Ephesians 6, we are instructed to take the Sword of the Spirit, which is the Word of God, and **pray at all times—on every occasion, in every season—in the Spirit, with all [manner of] prayer and entreaty** (Eph. 6:18 AMP).

In 1 Timothy 2 we are admonished and urged that **petitions, prayers, intercessions and thanksgiv-ings be offered on behalf of all men** (1 Tim. 2:1 AMP). *Prayer is our responsibility.*

Prayer must be the foundation of every Christian endeavor. Any failure is a prayer failure. We are *not* to be ignorant concerning God's Word. God desires for His people to be successful, to be filled with a full, deep and clear knowledge of His will (His Word) and to bear fruit in every good work. (Col. 1:9-13.) We then bring honor and glory to Him. (John 15:8.) He desires that we know how to pray, for **the prayer of the upright is his delight** (Prov. 15:8).

Our Father has not left us helpless. Not only has He given us His Word, but also He has given us the Holy Spirit to help our infirmities when we know not how to pray as we ought. (Rom. 8:26.) Praise God! Our Father has provided His people with every possible avenue to ensure their complete and total victory in this life in the name of our Lord Jesus. (1 John 5:3-5.)

We pray to the Father, in the name of Jesus, through the Holy Spirit, according to the Word!

Using God's Word on purpose, specifically, in prayer is one means of prayer, and it is a most effective and accurate means. Jesus said, **The words (truths) that I have been speaking to you are spirit and life** (John 6:63 AMP).

When Jesus faced Satan in the wilderness, He said, "It is written...it is written...it is written." We are to live, be upheld and be sustained by every Word that proceeds from the mouth of God. (Matt. 4:4.)

James, by the Spirit, admonishes that we do not have, because we do not ask. We ask and receive not, because we ask amiss. (James 4:2,3.) We must heed that admonishment now, for we are to become experts in prayer, rightly dividing the Word of Truth. (2 Tim. 2:15.)

Using the Word in prayer is *not* taking it out of context, for His Word in us is the key to answered prayer—to prayer that brings results. He is able to do exceedingly abundantly above all we ask or think, according to the power that works in us. (Eph. 3:20.) The power lies within God's Word. It is anointed by the Holy Spirit. The Spirit of God does not lead us apart from the Word, for the Word is of the Spirit of God. We apply that Word personally to ourselves and to others—not adding to or taking from it—in the name of Jesus. We apply the Word to the *now*—to those things, circumstances and situations facing each of us *now.*

Paul was very specific and definite in his praying. The first chapters of Ephesians, Philippians, Colossians and 2 Thessalonians are examples of how Paul prayed for believers. There are numerous others. *Search them out.* Paul wrote under the inspiration of the Holy Spirit. We can use these Spirit-given prayers today!

In 2 Corinthians 1:11, 2 Corinthians 9:14 and Philippians 1:4, we see examples of how believers prayed one for another—putting others first in their prayer lives with *joy.* Our faith does work by love. (Gal. 5:6.) We grow spiritually as we reach out to help others—praying for and with them and holding out to them the Word of Life. (Phil. 2:16.)

Man is a spirit, he has a soul and he lives in a body. (1 Thess. 5:23.) In order to operate successfully, each of these three parts must be fed properly. The soul, or intellect, feeds on intellectual food to produce intellectual strength. The body feeds on physical food to produce physical strength. The spirit—the heart, or inward man—is the real you, the part that has been reborn in Christ Jesus. It must feed on spirit food, which is God's Word, in order to produce and develop faith. As we feast upon God's Word, our minds become renewed with His Word, and we have a fresh mental and spiritual attitude. (Eph. 4:23,24.)

Likewise, we are to present our bodies a living sacrifice, holy, acceptable unto God (Rom. 12:1) and not let our bodies dominate us but bring them into subjection to the spirit man. (1 Cor. 9:27.) God's Word is healing and health to all our flesh. (Prov. 4:22.) Therefore, God's Word affects each part of us— spirit, soul and body. We become vitally united to the Father, to Jesus and to the Holy Spirit—one with Them. (John 16:13-15, John 17:21, Col. 2:10.)

Purpose to hear, accept and welcome the Word, and it will takes root within your spirit and save your soul. Believe the Word, speak the Word and act on the Word—it is a creative force. The Word is a double-edged sword. Often it places a demand on you to change attitudes and behaviors toward the person for whom you are praying.

Be doers of the Word, and not hearers only, deceiving your own selves. (James 1:22.) Faith without works, or corresponding action, is *dead*. (James 2:17.) Don't be mental assenters—those who agree that the Bible is true but never act on it. *Real faith is acting on God's Word now.* We cannot build faith without practicing the Word. We cannot develop an effective prayer life that is anything but empty words unless God's Word actually has a part in our lives. We are to hold fast to our *confession* of the Word's truthfulness. Our Lord Jesus is the High Priest of our confession (Heb. 3:1), and He is the Guarantee of a better agreement—a more excellent and advantageous covenant. (Heb. 7:22.)

Prayer does not cause faith to work, but faith causes prayer to work. Therefore, any prayer problem is a lack of knowledge or a problem of doubt—doubting the integrity of the Word and the ability of God to stand behind His promises, or the statements of fact, in the Word.

We can spend fruitless hours in prayer if our hearts are not prepared beforehand. Preparation of the heart, the spirit, comes from meditation in the Father's Word—meditation on who we are in Christ, what He is to us and what the Holy Spirit can mean to us as we become God-inside minded. As God told Joshua, as we meditate on the Word day and night, and do according to all that is written, then shall we make our way prosperous and have good success. (Josh. 1:8.) We are to attend to God's Word, submit to His sayings, keep them in the center of our hearts and put away contrary talk. (Prov. 4:20-24.)

The Holy Spirit is a Divine Helper and He will direct our prayer, and help us pray when we don't know how. When we use God's Word in prayer, this is *not* something we just rush through uttering once, and we are finished. Do *not* be mistaken. There is nothing "magical" or "manipulative" about it—no set pattern or device in order to satisfy what we want or think out of our flesh. Instead, we are holding God's Word before Him. Jesus said for us to ask the Father in His name.

We expect His divine intervention, while we choose not to look at the things that are seen but at the things that are unseen, for the things that are seen are subject to change. (2 Cor. 4:18.)

Prayer based upon the Word rises above the senses, contacts the Author of the Word and sets His spiritual laws into motion. It is not just saying prayers that gets results, but it is spending time with the Father, learning His wisdom, drawing on His strength, being filled with His quietness and basking in His love that bring results to our prayers. Praise the Lord!

The prayers in this book are designed to teach and train you in the art of prayer. As you pray them, you will be reinforcing the prayer armor which we have been instructed to put on in Ephesians 6:11. The fabric from which the armor is made is the Word of God. We are to live by every word that proceeds from the mouth of God. We desire the whole counsel of God, because we know it changes us. By receiving that counsel, you will be **transformed (changed) by the [entire] renewal of your mind—by its new ideals and attitude—so that you may prove [for yourselves] what is the good and acceptable and perfect will of God, even the thing which is good and acceptable and perfect [in His sight for you]** (Rom. 12:2 AMP).

The Personal Prayers (Part I) may be used as intercessory prayer by simply praying them in the third person, changing the pronouns *I* or *we* to the name of the person for whom you are interceding and adjusting the verbs accordingly. The Holy Spirit is your Helper. Remember that you cannot control another's will, but your prayers prepare the way for the individual to hear truth and understand truth.

An often-asked question is "How many times should I pray the same prayer?"

The answer is simple: You pray until you know that the answer is fixed in your heart. After that, you need to repeat the prayer whenever adverse circumstances or long delays cause you to be tempted to doubt that your prayer has been heard and your request granted. Reaffirming your faith enforces the triumphant victory of our Lord Jesus Christ.

The Word of God is your weapon against the temptation to lose heart and grow weary in your prayer life. When that Word of promise becomes fixed in your heart, you will find yourself praising, giving glory to God for the answer, even when the only evidence you have of that answer is your own faith.

Another question often asked is "When we repeat prayers more than once, aren't we praying 'vain repetitions'?"

Obviously, such people are referring to the admonition of Jesus when He told His disciples: **And when you pray do not (multiply words, repeating the same ones over and over, and) heap up phrases as the Gentiles do, for they think they will be heard for their much speaking** (Matt. 6:7 AMP). Praying the Word of God is not praying the kind of prayer that the "heathen" pray. You will note in 1 Kings 18:25-29 the manner of prayer that was offered to the gods who could not hear. That is not the way you and I pray. The words that we speak are not vain, but they are spirit and life and mighty through God to the pulling down of strongholds. We have a God Whose eyes are over the righteous and Whose ears are open to us: When we pray, He hears us.

You are the righteousness of God in Christ Jesus, and your prayers will avail much. They will bring salvation to the sinner, deliverance to the oppressed, healing to the sick and prosperity to the poor. They will usher in the next move of God on the earth. In addition to affecting outward circumstances and other people, your prayers will also effect you.

In the very process of praying, you will be changed as you go from faith to faith and from glory to glory.

As a Christian, you should make your first priority to love the Lord your God with your entire being, and your neighbor as yourself. You are called to be an intercessor, a man or woman of prayer. You are to seek the face of the Lord as you inquire, listen, meditate and consider in the temple of the Lord.

As one of "God's set-apart ones," you have been given the same commission as every other true believer: **Seek ye first the kingdom of God, and his righteousness; and all these things shall be added unto you** (Matt. 6:33).

Personal Confessions

Jesus is Lord over my spirit, my soul and my body. (Phil. 2:9-11.)

Jesus has been made unto me wisdom, righteousness, sanctification and redemption. I can do all things through Christ, Who strengthens me. (1 Cor. 1:30, Phil. 4:13.)

The Lord is my shepherd. I do not want. My God supplies all my need according to His riches in glory in Christ Jesus. (Ps. 23, Phil. 4:19.)

I do not fret or have anxiety about anything. I do not have a care. (Phil. 4:6; 1 Pet. 5:6,7.)

I am the Body of Christ. I am redeemed from the curse, because Jesus bore my sicknesses and carried my diseases in His own body. By His stripes I am healed. I forbid any sickness or disease to operate in my body. Every organ, every tissue of my body functions in the perfection in which God created it to function. I honor God and bring glory to Him in my body. (Gal. 3:13, Matt. 8:17, 1 Pet. 2:24, 1 Cor. 6:20.)

I have the mind of Christ and hold the thoughts, feelings and purposes of His heart. (1 Cor. 2:16.)

I am a believer and not a doubter. I hold fast to my confession of faith. I decide to walk by faith and practice faith. My faith comes by hearing and hearing by the Word of God. Jesus is the author and the developer of my faith. (Heb. 4:14, Heb. 11:6, Rom. 10:17, Heb. 12:2.)

The love of God has been shed abroad in my heart by the Holy Spirit, and His love abides in me richly. I keep myself in the Kingdom of light, in love, in the Word; and the wicked one touches me not. (Rom. 5:5, 1 John 4:16, 1 John 5:18.)

I tread upon serpents and scorpions and over all the power of the enemy. I take my shield of faith and quench his every fiery dart. Greater is He Who is in me than he who is in the world. (Ps. 91:13, Eph. 6:16, 1 John 4:4.)

I am delivered from this present evil world. I am seated with Christ in heavenly places. I reside in the Kingdom of God's dear Son. The law of the Spirit of life in Christ Jesus has made me free from the law of sin and death. (Gal. 1:4, Eph. 2:6, Col. 1:13, Rom. 8:2.)

I fear not, for God has given me a spirit of power, of love and of a sound mind. God is on my side. (2 Tim. 1:7, Rom. 8:31.)

I hear the voice of the Good Shepherd. I hear my Father's voice, and the voice of a stranger I will not follow. I roll my works upon the Lord. I commit and trust them wholly to Him. He will cause my thoughts to become agreeable to His will, and so shall my plans be established and succeed. (John 10:27, Prov. 16:3.)

I am a world overcomer because I am born of God. I represent the Father and Jesus well. I am a useful member in the Body of Christ. I am His workmanship, re-created in Christ Jesus. My Father God is all the while effectually at work in me both to will and do His good pleasure. (1 John 5:4,5; Eph. 2:10; Phil. 2:13.)

I let the Word dwell in me richly. He Who began a good work in me will continue until the day of Christ. (Col. 3:16, Phil. 1:6.)

Prayers of Praise

O magnify the Lord with me, and let us exalt His name together.

As for God, His way is perfect! The Word of the Lord is tested and tried; He is a shield to all those who take refuge and put their trust in Him.

Let the words of my mouth and the meditation of my heart be acceptable in Your sight, O Lord, my firm, impenetrable rock and my redeemer.

Your Word has revived me and given me life.

Forever, O Lord, Your Word is settled in heaven.

Your Word is a lamp to my feet and a light to my path.

The sum of Your Word is truth and every one of Your righteous decrees endures forever.

I will worship toward Your Holy Temple and praise Your name for Your loving-kindness and for Your truth and faithfulness, for You have exalted above all else Your name and Your Word, and You have magnified Your Word above all Your name!

Let my prayer be set forth as incense before You, the lifting up of my hands as the evening sacrifice. Set a guard, O Lord, before my mouth; keep watch at the door of my lips.

He who brings an offering of praise and thanksgiving honors and glorifies Me; and he who orders his way aright—who prepares the way that I may show him—to him I will demonstrate the salvation of God.

My mouth shall be filled with Your praise and with Your honor all the day.

Because Your loving-kindness is better than life, my lips shall praise You. So will I bless You while I live; I will lift up my hands in Your name.

Your testimonies also are my delight and my counselors.

Scripture References (AMP)

Psalm 34:3	Psalm 138:2
Psalm 18:30	Psalm 142:2,3
Psalm 19:14	Psalm 50:23
Psalm 119:50	Psalm 71:8
Psalm 119:89	Psalm 63:3,4
Psalm 119:105	Psalm 119:24
Psalm 119:160	

PART I

Personal Prayers

Prayers of Commitment

1

To Walk in the Word

*F*ather, in the name of Jesus, *I commit myself to walk in the Word.* Your Word living in me produces Your life in this world. I recognize that Your Word is integrity itself—steadfast, sure, eternal—and I trust my life to its provisions.

You have sent your Word forth into my heart. I let it dwell in me richly in all wisdom. I meditate in it day and night so that I may diligently act on it. The Incorruptible Seed, the Living Word, the Word of Truth, is abiding in my spirit. That Seed is growing mightily in me now, producing Your nature, Your life. It is my counsel, my shield, my buckler, my powerful weapon in battle. The Word is a lamp to my feet and a light to my path. It makes my way plain before me. I do not stumble, for my steps are ordered in the Word.

The Holy Spirit leads and guides me into all the Truth. He gives me understanding, discernment and comprehension so that I am preserved from the snares of the evil one.

I delight myself in You and Your Word. Because of that, You put Your desires within my heart. I commit my way unto You, and You bring it to pass. I am confident that You are at work in me now both to will and to do all Your good pleasure.

I exalt Your Word, hold it in high esteem and give it first place. *I make my schedule around Your Word.* I make the Word final authority to settle all questions that confront me. I choose to agree with the Word of God, and I choose to disagree with any thoughts, conditions or circumstances contrary to Your Word. I boldly and confidently say that my heart is fixed and established on the solid foundation—the living Word of God!

Scripture References

Hebrews 4:12	1 Peter 3:12
Colossians 3:16	Colossians 4:2
Joshua 1:8	Ephesians 6:10
1 Peter 1:23	Luke 18:1
Psalm 91:4	James 5:16
Psalm 119:105	Psalm 37:4,5
Psalm 37:23	Philippians 2:13
Colossians 1:9	2 Corinthians 10:5
John 16:13	Psalm 112:7,8

2

To Be God-Inside Minded

I am a spirit being learning to live in a natural world. I have a soul and I live in a physical body. I am in the world but I am not of the world. God of peace, I ask you to sanctify me in every way, and may my whole spirit and soul and body be kept blameless until that day when our Lord Jesus Christ comes again. Father, you called me, and you are completely dependable. You said it and you will do this. Thank you for the Spirit who guides me into all truth through my regenerated human spirit.

Lord, your searchlight penetrates my human spirit, exposing every hidden motive. You actually gave me your Spirit (not the world's spirit) so I can know the wonderful things You have given us. I am a child of God, born of the Spirit of God, filled with the Spirit of God, and led by the Spirit of God. I listen to my heart as I look to my spirit inside me.

Thank you, Holy Spirit, for directing me and illuminating my mind. You lead me in the way I should go in all the affairs of life. You lead me by an inward witness. The eyes of my understanding are being enlightened. Wisdom is in my inward parts. God's love is perfected in me. I have a unction from the Holy One.

Father, I am becoming spirit-conscious. I listen to the voice of my spirit and obey what my spirit tells me. My spirit is controlled by the Holy Spirit and dominates me, for I walk not after the flesh, but after the spirit. I examine my leading in the light of the Word.

I trust in You, Lord, with all my heart and lean not to my own understanding. In all my ways I acknowledge you, and you direct my paths. I walk in the light of the Word.

Holy Spirit, You are my Counselor teaching me to educate, train and develop my human spirit. The Word of God shall not depart out of my mouth. I meditate therein day and night. Therefore I shall make my way prosperous, and I will have good success in life. I am a doer of the Word and put Your Word first.

Scripture References

I Thessalonians 5:23-24

John 16:13

Proverbs 20:27 NLT

I Corinthians 2:12 NLT

Romans 8:14,16

John 3:6,7

Ephesians 5:18

Isaiah 48:17

Ephesians 1:18

I John 4:12

I John 2:20

Romans 8:1

Proverbs 3:5,6

Psalm 119:105

John 14:26

Joshua 1:8

James 1:22

3

To Rejoice in the Lord

*F*ather, this is the day the Lord has made. I rejoice and I am glad in it! I rejoice in You always. And again I say, I rejoice. I delight myself in You, Lord. Happy am I because God is my Lord!

Father, thank you for loving me and rejoicing over me with joy. Hallelujah! I am redeemed. I come with singing, and everlasting joy is upon my head. I obtain joy and gladness, and sorrow and sighing flee away. That spirit of rejoicing, joy and laughter is my heritage. Where the Spirit of the Lord is there is liberty—emancipation from bondage, freedom. I walk in that liberty.

Father, I praise You with joyful lips. I am ever filled and stimulated with the Holy Spirit. I speak out in psalms and hymns and make melody with all my heart to You, Lord. My happy heart is a good medicine, and my cheerful mind works healing. The light in my eyes rejoices the heart of others. I have a good report. My countenance radiates the joy of the Lord.

Father, I thank You that I bear much prayer fruit. I ask in Jesus' name, and I will receive so that my joy (gladness, delight) may be full, complete and overflowing. The joy of the Lord is my *strength*. Therefore, I count it all joy, all strength, when I encounter tests or trials of any sort, because I am strong in You, Father.

I have the *victory* in the name of Jesus. Satan is under my feet. I am not moved by adverse circumstances. I have been made the righteousness of God in Christ Jesus. I dwell in the Kingdom of God and have peace and joy in the Holy Spirit! Praise the Lord!

Scripture References

Psalm 118:24	Philippians 4:8
Philippians 4:4	Proverbs 15:13
Philippians 3:1	John 15:7,8
Psalm 144:15	John 16:23
Zephaniah 3:17	Nehemiah 8:10
Isaiah 51:11	James 1:2
2 Corinthians 3:17	Ephesians 6:10
James 1:25	1 John 5:4
Psalm 63:5	Ephesians 1:22
Ephesians 5:18,19	2 Corinthians 5:7
Proverbs 17:22	2 Corinthians 5:21
Proverbs 15:30	Romans 14:17

4

To Walk in God's Wisdom and His Perfect Will

*L*ord and God, You are worthy to receive glory and honor and power, for You created all things, and by Your will they were created and have their being. You adopted me as Your child through Jesus Christ, in accordance with Your pleasure and will. I pray that I may be active in sharing my faith, so that I will have a full understanding of every good thing I have in Christ.

Father, I ask You to give me a complete under-standing of what You want to do in my life, and I ask You to make me wise with spiritual wisdom. Then the way I live will always honor and please You, and I will continually do good kind things for others. All the while, I will learn to know You better and better.

I roll my works upon You, Lord, and You make my thoughts agreeable to Your will, and so my plans are established and succeed. You direct my steps and make them sure. I understand and firmly grasp what the will of the Lord is, for I am not vague, thoughtless or foolish. I stand firm and mature in spiritual growth, convinced and fully assured in everything willed by God.

Father, You have destined and appointed me to come progressively to know Your will—that is, to perceive, to recognize more strongly and clearly and to become better and more intimately acquainted with Your will. I thank You, Father, for the Holy Spirit, Who abides permanently in me and Who guides me into all the Truth—the whole, full Truth—and speaks whatever He hears from the Father and announces and declares to me the things that are to come. I have the mind of Christ and hold the thoughts, feelings and purposes of His heart.

So, Father, I have entered into that blessed rest by adhering to, trusting in and relying on You in the name of Jesus. Hallelujah!

Scripture References

Revelation 4:11 NIV   Colossians 4:12 AMP

Ephesians 1:5 NIV   Acts 22:14

Colossians 1:9,10 NLT   I Corinthians 2:16 AMP

Proverbs 16:3,9 AMP   Hebrews 4:10

Ephesians 5:16 AMP

5

To Walk in Love

*F*ather, in Jesus' name, I thank You that the love of God has been poured forth into my heart by the Holy Spirit, Who has been given to me. I keep and treasure Your Word. The love of and for You, Father, has been perfected and completed in me, and perfect love casts out all fear.

Father, I am Your child, and *I commit to walk in the God kind of love.* I endure long and am patient, and kind. I am never envious and never boil over with jealousy. I am not boastful or vainglorious, and I do not display myself haughtily. I am not rude and unmannerly, and I do not act unbecomingly. I do not insist on my own rights or my own way, for I am not self-seeking, touchy, fretful or resentful. I take no account of an evil done to me and pay no attention to a suffered wrong. I do not rejoice at injustice and unrighteousness, but I rejoice when right and truth prevail. I bear up under anything and everything that comes. I am ever ready to believe the *best* of others. My hopes are fadeless under all circumstances. I endure everything without weakening because the love of God in me never fails.

Father, I *bless* and *pray* for those who persecute me—who are cruel in their attitude toward me. I bless them and do not curse them. Therefore, my love abounds yet more and more in knowledge and in all judgment. I approve things that are excellent. I am sincere and *without offense* till the day of Christ. I am filled with the fruits of righteousness.

Everywhere I go I commit to plant seeds of love. I thank You, Father, for preparing hearts ahead of time to receive this love. I know that these seeds will produce Your love in the hearts to whom they are given.

Father, I thank You that as I flow in Your love and wisdom, people are being blessed by my life and ministry. Father, You make me to find favor, compassion, and loving-kindness with others (*name them*).

I am rooted deep in love and founded securely on love, knowing that You are on my side, and nothing is able to separate me from Your love, Father, which is in Christ Jesus my Lord. Thank You, Father, in Jesus' precious name. Amen.

Scripture References

Romans 5:5	Philippians 1:9-11
1 John 2:5	John 13:34
1 John 4:18	1 Corinthians 3:6
1 Corinthians 13:4-8	Daniel 1:9
Romans 12:14	Ephesians 3:17
Matthew 5:44	Romans 8:31,39

6

To Walk in Forgiveness

*F*ather, in the name of Jesus, I make a fresh commitment to You to live in peace and harmony, not only with the other brothers and sisters of the Body of Christ, but also with my friends, associates, neighbors and family.

Father, I repent of holding on to bad feelings toward others. I bind myself to godly repentance and loose myself from bitterness, resentment, envying, strife, and unkindness in any form. Father, I ask Your forgiveness for the sin of _____. By faith, I receive it, having assurance that I am cleansed from all unrighteousness through Jesus Christ. I ask You to forgive and release all who have wronged and hurt me. I forgive and release them. Deal with them in Your mercy and loving-kindness.

From this moment on, I purpose to walk in love, to seek peace, to live in agreement and to conduct myself toward others in a manner that is pleasing to You. I know that I have right standing with You and Your ears are attentive to my prayers.

It is written in Your Word that the love of God has been poured forth into my heart by the Holy Ghost, Who is given to me. I believe that love flows forth into the lives of everyone I know, that I may be filled with and abound in the fruits of righteousness, which bring glory and honor unto You, Lord, in Jesus' name. So be it!

Scripture References

Romans 12:16-18

Romans 12:10

Philippians 2:2

Ephesians 4:31

Ephesians 4:27

John 1:9

Mark 11:25

Ephesians 4:32

1 Peter 3:8,11,12

Colossians 1:10

Romans 5:5

Philippians 1:9,11

7

To Watch What You Say

*F*ather, today, I make a commitment to You in the name of Jesus. I turn from idle words and foolishly talking things that are contrary to my true desire to myself and toward others. Your Word says that the tongue defiles, that the tongue sets on fire the course of nature, that the tongue is set on fire of hell.

In the name of Jesus, I submit to godly wisdom that I might learn to control my tongue. I am determined that hell will not set my tongue on fire. I renounce, reject and repent of every word that has ever proceeded out of my mouth against You, God, and Your operation. I cancel its power and dedicate my mouth to speak excellent and right things. My mouth shall utter truth.

Because I am the righteousness of God in Christ Jesus, I set the course of my life for obedience, for abundance, for wisdom, for health and for joy. Set a guard over my mouth, O Lord, keep watch over the door of my lips. Then . . . words of my mouth and my deeds shall show forth Your righteousness and Your salvation all of my days. I purpose to guard my mouth and my tongue that I might keep myself from calamity.

Father, Your Words are top priority to me. They are spirit and life. I let the Word dwell in me richly in all wisdom. The ability of God is released within me by the words of my mouth and by the Word of God. I speak Your words out of my mouth. They are alive in me. You are alive and working in me. So, I can boldly say that my words are words of faith, words of power, words of love and words of life. They produce good things in my life and in the lives of others. Because I choose Your words for my lips, I choose Your will for my life, in Jesus' name.

Scripture References

Ephesians 5:4	Proverbs 21:23
2 Timothy 2:16	Ephesians 4:27
James 3:6	James 1:6
Proverbs 8:6,7	John 6:63
2 Corinthians 5:21	Colossians 3:16
Proverbs 4:23	Philemon 6

8

To Live Free From Worry

*F*ather, I thank You that I have been delivered from the power of darkness and translated into the Kingdom of Your dear Son. *I commit to live free from worry, in the name of Jesus,* for the law of the Spirit of life in Christ Jesus has made me *free* from the law of sin and death.

I humble myself under Your mighty hand, that in due time You may exalt me. I cast the whole of my cares (*name them*)—all my anxieties, all my worries, all my concerns—once and for all, on You. You care for me affectionately and care about me watchfully. You sustain me. You will never allow the consistently righteous to be moved—made to slip, fall or fail!

Father, I delight myself in You, and You perfect that which concerns me.

I cast down imaginations (reasonings) and every high thing that exalts itself against the knowledge of You, and bring into captivity every thought to the obedience of Christ. I lay aside every weight and the sin of worry which does try so easily to beset me. I run with patience the race that is set before me, looking unto Jesus, the Author and Finisher of my faith.

I thank You, Father, that You are able to keep that which I have committed unto You. I think on (fix my mind on) those things that are true, honest, just, pure, lovely, of good report, virtuous and deserving of praise. I will not let my heart be troubled. I abide in Your words, and Your words abide in me. Therefore, Father, I do *not* forget what manner of person I am. I look into the perfect law of liberty and continue therein, being *not* a forgetful hearer, but a *doer of the Word* and thus blessed in my doing!

Thank You, Father. *I am carefree.* I walk in that peace which passes all understanding, in Jesus' name!

Scripture References

Colossians 1:13	Hebrews 12:1,2
Romans 8:2	2 Timothy 1:12
1 Peter 5:6,7	Philippians 4:8
Psalm 55:22	John 14:1
Psalm 138:8	James 1:22-25
2 Corinthians 10:5	Philippians 4:6

9

To Receive Jesus As Savior and Lord

*F*ather, it is written in Your Word that if I confess with my mouth that Jesus is Lord and believe in my heart that You have raised Him from the dead, I shall be saved. Therefore, Father, I confess that Jesus is my Lord. I make Him Lord of my life right now. I believe in my heart that You raised Jesus from the dead. I renounce my past life with Satan and close the door to any of his devices.

I thank You for forgiving me of all my sin. Jesus is my Lord, and I am a new creation. Old things have passed away. Now all things become new in Jesus' name. Amen.

Scripture References

John 3:16

John 6:37

John 10:10b

Romans 3:23

2 Corinthians 5:19

John 16:8,9

Romans 5:8

John 14:6

Romans 10:9,10

Romans 10:13

Ephesians 2:1-10

2 Corinthians 5:17

John 1:12

2 Corinthians 5:21

10

To Receive the Infilling of the Holy Spirit

My heavenly Father, I am Your child, for I believe in my heart that Jesus has been raised from the dead and I have confessed Him as my Lord.

Jesus said, "How much more shall your heavenly Father give the Holy Spirit to those who ask Him." I ask You now, in the name of Jesus, to fill me with the Holy Spirit. I step into the fullness and power that I desire in the name of Jesus. I confess that I am a Spirit-filled Christian. As I yield my vocal organs, I expect to speak in tongues, for the Spirit gives me utterance in the name of Jesus. Praise the Lord!

Scripture References

John 14:16,17	Acts 10:44-46
Luke 11:13	Acts 19:2,5,6
Acts 1:8a	1 Corinthians 14:2-15
Acts 2:4	1 Corinthians 14:18,27
Acts 2:32,33,39	Ephesians 6:18
Acts 8:12-17	Jude 1:20

Prayers for
Personal
Concerns

11

Boldness

*F*ather, in the name of Jesus, I am of good courage, I pray that You grant to me that with all *boldness* I speak forth Your Word. I pray that freedom of utterance be given me, that I may open my mouth to proclaim *boldly* the mystery of the good news of the Gospel—that I may declare it *boldly* as I ought to do.

Father, I believe I receive that *boldness* now in the name of Jesus. Therefore, I have *boldness* to enter into the Holy of Holies by the blood of Jesus. Because of my faith in Him, I dare to have the *boldness* (courage and confidence) of free access—an unreserved approach to You with freedom and without fear. I can draw fearlessly and confidently and *boldly* near to Your throne of grace and receive mercy and find grace to help in good time for my every need. I am *bold* to pray. I come to the throne of God with my petitions, and for others who do not know how to ascend to the throne.

I will be *bold* toward Satan, demons, evil spirits, sickness, disease and poverty, for Jesus is the Head of all rule and authority—of every angelic principality and power. Disarming those who were ranged against us, Jesus made a *bold* display and public example of them, triumphing over them. I am *bold* to declare that Satan is a defeated foe. Let God arise and His enemies be scattered

I take comfort and am encouraged and confidently and *boldly* say, "The Lord is my Helper, I will not be seized with alarm—I will not fear or dread or be terrified. What can man do to me?" I dare to proclaim the Word toward heaven, toward hell and toward earth. I am *bold* as a lion, for I have been made the righteousness of God in Christ Jesus. I am complete in Him! Praise the name of Jesus!

Scripture References

Psalm 27:14

Acts 4:29

Ephesians 6:19,20

Mark 11:23,24

Hebrews 10:19 AMP

Ephesians 3:12

Hebrews 4:16

Colossians 2:10,15

Hebrews 13:6

Proverbs 28:1

2 Corinthians 5:21

12

Husbands

*F*ather, in the beginning You provided a partner for man. Now, I have found a wife to be my partner, and I have obtained favor from the Lord. I will not let mercy and truth forsake me. I bind them around my neck, and write them on the tablet of my heart, and so I find favor and high esteem in the sight of God and man.

In the name of Jesus, I purpose to provide leadership to my wife the way Christ does to His church, not by domineering but by cherishing. I will go all out in my love for her, exactly as Christ did for the church— a love marked by giving, not getting. We are the body of Christ, and when I love my wife, I love myself.

It is my desire to give my wife what is due to her, and I purpose to share my personal rights with her. Father, I am neither anxious nor intimidated, but a good husband to my wife. I honor her, and delight in her. In the new life of God's grace, we are equals. I purpose to treat my wife as an equal so that our prayers will be answered.

LORD, I delight greatly in Your commandments, and my descendants will be mighty on earth, and the generation of the upright will be blessed. Wealth and riches will be in our house, and my righteousness will endure forever.

In the name of Jesus. Amen

Scripture References

Matthew 18:18   Ephesians 5:22-33 THE MESSAGE

Genesis 2:18 NEB*   I Corinthians 7:3-5**

Proverbs 18:22 NKJ   I Peter 3:7-9 THE MESSAGE

Proverbs 3:3-4 NKJ   Psalm 112 NKJ

Proverbs 31:28-31 NLB

* *(The Bible from 26 Translations,* © Mathis Publishers, Inc., Moss Point, MS)

** *The New Testament in Modern English,* J. B. Phillips

13

Wives

*I*n the name of Jesus I cultivate inner beauty, the gentle, gracious kind that God delights in. I choose to be a good, loyal wife to my husband, and address him with respect. I will not be over-anxious and intimidated. I purpose to be by God's grace agreeable, sympathetic, loving, compassionate and humble. I will be a blessing and also receive blessings.

By the grace of God, I yield to the constant ministry of transformation by the Holy Spirit. I am being transformed into a gracious woman who retains honor, and a virtuous woman who is a crown to my husband. I purpose to walk wisely that I might build my house. House and riches are the inheritance of fathers: and a prudent wife is from the Lord. In Christ I have redemption through His blood, the forgiveness of sins, according to the riches of His grace which He made to abound toward me in all wisdom and prudence.

Holy Spirit, I ask You to help me understand and support my husband in ways that show my support for Christ. *Teach me to function so that I preserve my own personality while responding to his desires. We are one flesh, and I realize that this unity of persons that preserves individuality is a mystery, but that is how it is when we are united to Christ. So I will keep on loving my husband and let the miracle keep happening!

Just as my husband gives me what is due to me, I seek to be fair to my husband. I share my rights with my husband.

Strength and dignity are my clothing and my position in my household is strong. My family is in readiness for the future. The bread of idleness (gossip, discontent, and self-pity) I will not eat. I choose to conduct the affairs of my household wisely realizing that wisdom from above is pure, peaceable, gentle, willing to yield, full of mercy and good fruits, without partiality and without hypocrisy. Amen.

Scripture References

Matthew 16:19 NKJ	Proverbs 14:1
I Peter 3:1-5, 8-9	Proverbs 19:14
THE MESSAGE	Ephesians 1:7-8 NKJ
Psalm 51:10 NKJ	Ephesians 5:22-33*
II Corinthians 3:18	I Corinthians 7:2-5**
Proverbs 11:16	Proverbs 31:25, 26, 27 AMP
Proverbs 12:4	James 3:17-18 NKJ

* *The Message and Paraphrase The Heart of Paul*, Ben Campbell Johnson, © 1976 Ben Campbell Johnson, A Great Love, Inc. Toccoa, GA 30577

** *The New Testament in Modern English*, J.B. Phillips

14

Harmonious Marriage

*F*ather, in the name of Jesus, it is written in Your Word that love is shed abroad in our hearts by the Holy Ghost, Who is given to us. Because You are in us, we acknowledge that love reigns supreme. We believe that love is displayed in full expression enfolding and knitting us together in truth, making us perfect for every good work to do Your will, working in us that which is pleasing in Your sight.

We live and conduct ourselves and our marriage honorably and becomingly. We esteem it as precious, worthy, and of great price. *We commit ourselves to live in mutual harmony and accord with one another,* delighting in each other, being of the same mind and united in spirit.

Father, we believe and say that we are gentle, compassionate, courteous, tenderhearted and humble-minded. We seek peace, and it keeps our hearts in quietness and assurance. Because we follow after love and dwell in peace, our prayers are not hindered in any way, in the name of Jesus. We are heirs together of the grace of God.

Our marriage grows stronger day by day in the bond of unity because it is founded on Your Word and rooted and grounded in Your love. Father, we thank You for the performance of it, in Jesus' name.

Scripture References

Romans 5:5	Ephesians 4:32
Philippians 1:9	Isaiah 32:17
Colossians 3:14	Philippians 4:7
Colossians 1:10	1 Peter 3:7
Philippians 2:13	Ephesians 3:17,18
Philippians 2:2	Jeremiah 1:12

15

Compatibility in Marriage

*F*ather, in the name of Jesus, the love of God is shed abroad in our hearts by the Holy Spirit who indwells us. Therefore my spouse and I are learning to endure long and are patient and kind, that we are never envious and never boil over with jealousy. We are not boastful or vainglorious, and we do not display ourselves haughtily. We are not conceited or arrogant and inflated with pride. We are not rude and unmannerly, and we do not act unbecomingly. We do not insist on our own rights or our own way, for we are not self-seeking or touchy or fretful or resentful. We take no account of the evil done to us and pay no attention to a suffered wrong. We do not rejoice at injustice and unrighteousness, but we rejoice when right and truth prevail.

We bear up under anything and everything that comes. We are ever ready to believe the best of each other. Our hopes are fadeless under all circumstances. We endure everything without weakening. *Our love never fails*—it never fades out or becomes obsolete or comes to an end.

We are no longer children tossed to and fro, carried about with every wind of doctrine, but we speak the truth in love, dealing truly, and living truly. We are enfolded in love growing up in every way and in all things. We esteem and delight in one another, forgiving one another readily and freely as God in Christ has forgiven us. We are imitators of God and copy His example as well-beloved children imitate their father.

Thank You, Father, that our marriage grows stronger each day because it is founded on Your Word and on Your kind of love. We give You the praise for it all, Father, in the name of Jesus.

Scripture References

1 Corinthians 13:4-8 AMP   Ephesians 4:15,32

1 Corinthians 14:1   Ephesians 5:1,2

16

The Children

*F*ather, in the name of Jesus, I pray and confess Your Word over my children and surround them with my faith—faith that You watch over Your Word to perform it! I confess and believe that my children are disciples of Christ, taught of the Lord and obedient to Your will. Great is the peace and undisturbed composure of my children because You, God, contend with that which contends with my children, and You give them safety and ease them.

Father, You will perfect that which concerns me. *I commit and cast the care of my children once and for all over on You, Father.* They are in Your hands, and I am positively persuaded that You are able to guard and keep that which I have committed to You. You are more than enough!

I confess that my children obey their parents in the Lord as His representatives, because this is just and right. My children, _____, honor, esteem and value as precious their parents; for this is the first commandment with a promise: that all may be well with my children and that they may live long on earth. I believe and confess that my children choose life and love You, Lord, obey Your voice and cling to You; for You are their life and the length of their days. Therefore, my children are the head and not the tail, and shall be above only and not beneath. They are blessed when they come in and when they go out.

I believe and confess that You give Your angels charge over my children to accompany and defend and preserve them in all their ways. You, Lord, are their refuge and fortress. You are their glory and the lifter of their heads.

As parents, we will not provoke, irritate, or fret our children. We will not be hard on them or harass them or cause them to become discouraged, sullen or morose or to feel inferior and frustrated. We will not break or wound their spirits, but we will rear them tenderly in the training, discipline, counsel and admonition of the Lord. We will train them in the way they should go, and when they are old they will not depart from it.

O Lord, my Lord, how excellent (majestic and glorious) is Your name in all the earth! You have set Your glory on or above the heavens. Out of the mouth of babes and unweaned infants You have established strength because of Your foes, that You might silence the enemy and the avenger. I sing praise to Your name, O Most High. *The enemy is turned back from my children in the name of Jesus!* They increase in wisdom and in favor with God and man.

Scripture References

Jeremiah 1:12	Psalm 91:11
Isaiah 54:13	Psalm 91:2
Isaiah 49:25	Psalm 3:3
1 Peter 5:7	Colossians 3:21
2 Timothy 1:12	Ephesians 6:4
Ephesians 6:1-3	Proverbs 22:6
Deuteronomy 30:19,20	Psalm 8:1,2
Deuteronomy 28:13	Psalm 9:2,3
Deuteronomy 28:3,6	Luke 2:52

17

The Home

*F*ather, I thank You that You have blessed me with all spiritual blessings in Christ Jesus.

Through skillful and godly wisdom is my house (my life, my home, my family) built, and by understanding it is established on a sound and good foundation. And by knowledge shall the chambers (of its every area) be filled with all precious and pleasant riches—great priceless treasure. The house of the uncompromisingly righteous shall stand. Prosperity and welfare are in my house in the name of Jesus.

My house is securely built. It is founded on a rock—revelation knowledge of Your Word, Father. Jesus is my Cornerstone. Jesus is Lord of my household. Jesus is our Lord—spirit, soul and body.

Whatever may be our task, we work at it heartily as something done for You, Lord, and not for men.

We love each other with the God kind of love, and we dwell in peace. My home is deposited into Your charge, entrusted to Your protection and care.

Father, as for me and my house we shall serve the Lord in Jesus' name. Hallelujah!

Scripture References

Ephesians 1:3	*Acts 16:31*
Proverbs 24:3,4	*Philippians 2:10,11*
Proverbs 15:6	*Colossians 3:23*
Proverbs 12:7	*Colossians 3:14,15*
Psalm 112:3	*Acts 20:32*
Luke 6:48	*Joshua 24:15*
Acts 4:11	

18

Prosperity

Father, I come to You in the name of Jesus, concerning my financial situation. You are a very present help in trouble, and You are more than enough. Your word declares that You shall supply all my need according to Your riches in glory by Christ Jesus.

(If you have not been giving tithes and offerings include the statement of repentance in your prayer.) Forgive me for robbing You in tithes and offerings. I repent, and purpose to bring all my tithes into the storehouse that there may be food in Your house. Thank You for wise financial counselors and teachers who are teaching me the principles of good stewardship.

Lord of hosts, You said, "Try me now in this, and You will open the windows of heaven and pour out for me such blessing that there will not be room enough to receive it." You will rebuke the devourer for my sake, and my heart is filled with thanksgiving.

Lord, my God, I shall remember that it is You who gives me the power to get wealth that You may establish Your covenant. In the name of Jesus, I worship You only, and I will have no others gods before You.

You are able to make all grace – every favor and earthly blessing – come to me in abundance, so that I am always, and in all circumstances furnished in abundance for every good work and charitable donation. Amen.

Scripture References

Psalm 56:1   Deuteronomy 8:18-19

Philippians 4:19   2 Corinthians 9:8 AMP

Malachi 3: 8-12

19

Dedication for Your Tithes

I profess this day unto the Lord God that I have come into the inheritance which the Lord swore to give me. I am in the land which You have provided for me in Jesus Christ, the Kingdom of Almighty God. I was a sinner serving Satan; he was my god. But I called upon the name of Jesus, and You heard my cry and delivered me into the Kingdom of Your dear Son.

Jesus, as my Lord and High Priest, I bring the first fruits of my income to You and worship the Lord my God with it.

I rejoice in all the good which You have given to me and my household. I have hearkened to the voice of the Lord my God and have done according to all that He has commanded me. Now look down from your holy habitation from heaven and bless me as You said in Your Word. I thank You, Father, in Jesus' name.

Scripture References

Deuteronomy 26:1,3,10,11,14,15   Colossians 1:13

Ephesians 2:1-5   Hebrews 3:1,7,8

20

Health and Healing

*F*ather, in the name of Jesus, I come before You asking You to heal me. It is written that the prayer of faith will save the sick, and the Lord will raise him up. And if I have committed sins, I will be forgiven. I let go of all unforgiveness, resentment, anger and bad feelings toward anyone.

My body is the temple of the Holy Spirit, and I desire to be in good health. I seek truth that will make me free – both spiritual and natural (*good eating habits, medications if necessary, and appropriate rest and exercise*). You bought me at a price, and I desire to glorify You in my spirit and my body – they both belong to You.

Thank You, Father, for sending Your Word to heal me and deliver me from all my destructions. Jesus, You are the Word who became flesh and dwelt among us. You bore my griefs (pains) and carried my sorrows (sickness). You were pierced through for my transgressions, crushed for my iniquities, the chastening for my well being fell upon You, and by Your scourging I am healed.

Father, I give attention to Your words, and incline my ear to Your sayings. I will not let them depart from my sight, but keep them in the midst of my heart. For they are my life and health to my whole body.

Since the Spirit of Him who raised Jesus from the dead dwells in me, He who raised Christ from the dead will also give life to my mortal body through His Spirit who dwells in me.

Thank You that I will prosper and be in health even as my soul prospers. Amen.

Scripture References

James 5:15 NKJ	Proverbs 4:21-22 NAS
I Corinthians 6:19-20	Psalm 103:3-5 NAS
Psalm 107:20	Romans 8:11 NKJ
John 1:14	III John 2
Isaiah 53:4-5 NAS	

21

Safety

*F*ather, in the name of Jesus, I thank You that You watch over Your Word to perform it. I thank You that I dwell in the secret place of the Most High and that I remain stable and fixed under the shadow of the Almighty, Whose power no foe can withstand.

Father, You are my refuge and my fortress. *No evil shall befall me—no accident shall overtake me—nor any plague or calamity come near my home.* You give Your angels special charge over me, to accompany and defend and preserve me in all my ways of obedience and service. They are encamped around about me.

Father, You are my confidence, firm and strong. You keep my foot from being caught in a trap or hidden danger. Father, You give me safety and ease me—*Jesus is my safety!*

Traveling—As I go, I say, "Let me pass over to the other side," and I have what I say. I walk on my way securely and in confident trust, for my heart and mind are firmly fixed and stayed on You, and I am kept in perfect peace.

Sleeping—Father, I sing for joy upon my bed because You sustain me. In peace I lie down and sleep, for You alone, Lord, make me dwell in safety. I lie down and I am not afraid. My sleep is sweet for You give blessings to me in sleep. Thank You, Father, in Jesus' name. Amen.

Continue to feast and meditate upon all of Psalm 91 for yourself and your loved ones!

Scripture References

Jeremiah 1:12	Proverbs 3:23
Psalm 91:1,2	Psalm 112:7
Psalm 91:10	Isaiah 26:3
Psalm 91:11	Psalm 149:5
Psalm 34:7	Psalm 3:5
Proverbs 3:26	Psalm 4:8
Isaiah 49:25	Proverbs 3:24
Mark 4:35	Psalm 127:2

22

Victory Over Fear

*F*ather, when I am afraid, I will put my confidence in You. Yes, I will trust your promises. And since I trust You, what can mere man do to me?

You have not given me a spirit of timidity, but of power and love and discipline (sound judgement). Therefore I am not ashamed of the testimony of my Lord. I have not received a spirit of slavery leading to fear again, but I have received a spirit of adoption as a son by which I cry out, "Abba! Father!"

Jesus, You delivered me who through fear of death had been living all my life as a slave to constant dread. I receive the gift You left to me – peace of mind and heart! And the peace you give isn't fragile like the peace the world gives. I cast away troubled thoughts and I choose not to be afraid. I believe in God, I believe also in You.

Lord, You are my light and my salvation, You protect me from danger – whom shall I fear? When evil men come to destroy me, they will stumble and fall! Yes, though a might army marches against me, my heart shall know no fear! I am confident that You will save me.

Thank you, Holy Spirit for bringing these things to my remembrance when I am tempted to be afraid. I will trust in my God. In the name of Jesus, I pray.

Scripture References

Psalm 56:3-5 TLB	*Hebrews 2:15 TLB*
II Timothy 1:7-8 NAS	*John 14:1,17 TLB*
Romans 8:15 NAS	*Psalm 27:1-3 TLB*

23

Victory Over Depression

*F*ather, You are my refuge and my high tower and my stronghold in times of trouble. I lean on and confidently put my trust in You, for You have not forsaken me. I seek You on the authority of Your Word and the right of my necessity. I praise You, the help of my countenance and my God.

Lord, You lift up those who are bowed down. Therefore, I am strong and my heart takes courage. I establish myself on righteousness—right standing in conformity with Your will and order. I am far even from the thought of oppression or destruction, for I fear not. I am far from terror, for it shall not come near me.

Father, You have thoughts and plans for my welfare and peace. *My mind is stayed on You,* for I stop allowing myself to be agitated and disturbed and intimidated and cowardly and unsettled.

In the name of Jesus I loose my mind from wrong thought patterns. I tear down strongholds that have protected bad perceptions about myself. I submit to You, Father, and resist fear, discouragement, self-pity and depression. I will not give place to the devil by harboring resentment and holding onto anger. I surround myself with songs and shouts of deliverance from depression, and will continue to be an over-comer by the word of my testimony and the blood of the Lamb.

Father, I thank You that I have been given a spirit of power and of love and of a calm and well-balanced mind. I have discipline and self-control. I have the mind of Christ and hold the thoughts, feelings and purposes of His heart. I have a fresh mental and spiritual attitude, for I am constantly renewed in the spirit of my mind with Your Word, Father.

Therefore, I brace up and reinvigorate and cut through and make firm and straight paths for my feet—safe and upright and happy paths that go in the right direction. I arise from the depression and prostration in which circumstances have kept me. I rise to new life, I shine and am radiant with the glory of the Lord.

Thank You, Father, in Jesus' name, that I am set free from every evil work. I praise You that the joy of the Lord is my strength and stronghold! Hallelujah!

Scripture References

Psalm 9:9,10

Psalm 42:5,11

Psalm 146:8

Psalm 31:22-24

Isaiah 35:3,4

Isaiah 54:14

Isaiah 50:10

Jeremiah 29:11-13

Isaiah 26:3

John 14:27

James 4:7

Ephesians 4:27

Luke 4:18,19

2 Timothy 1:7

1 Corinthians 2:16

Philippians 2:5

Ephesians 4:23,24

Hebrews 12:12,13

Isaiah 60:1

Galatians 1:4

Nehemiah 8:10

24

Victory in a Healthy Lifestyle

Father, I am your child and Jesus is Lord over my spirit, soul and body. I praise You because I am fearfully and wonderfully made; Your works are wonderful, I know that full well.

Lord, thank You for declaring Your plans for me—plans to prosper me and not to harm me, plans to give me hope and a future. I choose to renew my mind to your plans for a healthy lifestyle. You have abounded toward me in all prudence and wisdom. Therefore I give thought to my steps. Teach me knowledge and good judgement.

My body is for the Lord. So here's what I want to do with Your help, Father-God. I choose to take my everyday, ordinary life—my sleeping, eating, going-to-work, and walking-around life—and place it before You as an offering. Embracing what You do for me is the best thing I can do for You.

Christ the Messiah will be magnified and receive glory and praise in this body of mine and will be boldly exalted in my person. Thank You, Father, in Jesus name! Hallelujah! Amen.

Scripture References

Psalm 139:14	Psalms 119:66
Jeremiah 29:11	Romans 12:1 MSG
Proverbs 14:15	Philippians 1:20 AMP

25

In Court Cases

*F*ather, in the name of Jesus, it is written in Your Word to call on You and You will answer me and show me great and mighty things. I put You in remembrance of Your Word and thank You that You watch over it to perform it.

I say that no weapon formed against me shall prosper and any tongue that rises against me in judgment I shall show to be in the wrong. This peace, security and triumph over opposition is my inheritance as Your child. This is the righteousness which I obtain from You, Father, which You impart to me as my justification. I am far from even the thought of destruction, for I shall not fear and terror shall not come near me.

Father, You say You will establish me to the end—keep me steadfast, give me strength and guarantee my vindication; that is, be my warrant against all accusation or indictment. Father, You contend with those who contend with me, and You perfect that which concerns me. I dwell in the secret place of the Most High, and this secret place hides me from the strife of tongues, for a false witness who breathes out lies is an abomination to You.

I am a true witness, and all my words are upright and in right standing with You, Father. By my long forbearing and calmness of spirit the judge is persuaded, and my soft speech breaks down the most bonelike resistance. Therefore, I am not anxious beforehand how I shall reply in defense or what I am to say, for the Holy Spirit teaches me *in that very hour* and moment what I ought to say to those in the outside world. My speech is seasoned with salt.

As a child of the light, I enforce the triumphant victory of my Lord Jesus Christ in this situation knowing that all of heaven is backing me. I am strong in You, Lord, and in the power of your might. Thank You for the shield of faith that quenches every fiery dart of the enemy. I am increasing in wisdom and in stature and years, and in favor with You, Father and with man. Praise the Lord! Amen.

Scripture References

Jeremiah 33:3	Proverbs 6:19
Jeremiah 1:12	Proverbs 14:25
Isaiah 43:26	Proverbs 8:8
Isaiah 54:17	Proverbs 25:15
Isaiah 54:14	Luke 12:11,12
1 Corinthians 1:8	Colossians 4:6
Isaiah 49:25	Matthew 18:18
Psalm 138:8	Ephesians 6:10,16
Psalm 91:1	Luke 2:52
Psalm 31:20	

PART II

Intercessory Prayers

for Others

Prayers for God's People and Ministries

26

The Body of Christ

*F*ather, You put all things under the feet of Jesus and gave Him to be head over all things to the church which is His body, the fullness of Him who fills all in all. We were dead in trespasses and sins, but You made us alive! Christ is our peace, and we are no longer strangers and foreigners, but fellow citizens with the saints and members of the household of God. Jesus is our Cornerstone.

Father, You want us to grow up, to know the whole truth and tell it in love – like Christ in everything. We take our lead from Christ, Who is the source of everything we do. He keeps us in step with each other. His very breath and blood flow through us, nourishing us so that we will grow up healthy in God, robust in love.

May we be filled with the knowledge of Your will in all wisdom and spiritual understanding. As the elect of God, holy and beloved, we put on tender mercies, kindness, humility, meekness, longsuffering; bearing with one another, and forgiving one another. If we have a complaint against another; even as Christ forgave us, so we also must do. Above all things, we put on love, which is the bond of perfection, and let the peace of God rule in our hearts, to which also we were called in one body, and we are thankful.

Full of belief, confident that we're presentable inside and out, we keep a firm grip on the promises that keep us going. Father, You always keep Your Word. Now we will see how inventive we can be in encouraging love and helping out, not avoiding worshiping together as some do but spurring each other on, especially as we see the big Day approaching.

Since we are all called to travel on the same road and in the same direction, we will stay together, both outwardly and inwardly. We have one Master, one faith, one baptism, one God and Father of all, Who rules over all, works through all, and is present in all. Everything we are and think and do is permeated with Oneness.

Father, we commit to pray for one another, keeping our eyes open, and keeping each other's spirits up so that no one falls behind or drops out. Also, we pray for our spiritual leaders that they will know what to say and have the courage to say it at the right time.

We are one in the bonds of love, in the name of Jesus.

Scripture References

Ephesians 1:22-23 NKJ

Ephesians 4:15-16 THE MESSAGE

Colossians 3:12-15 NKJ

Hebrew 10:23-25 THE MESSAGE

Ephesians 4:4-6 THE MESSAGE

Ephesians 6:18-19 THE MESSAGE

27

Ministers

*F*ather, in the name of Jesus, we pray and confess that the Spirit of the Lord—the spirit of wisdom and understanding, the spirit of counsel and might, the spirit of knowledge—shall rest upon _____ . We pray that as Your Spirit rests upon _____ He will make him/her of quick understanding because You, Lord, have anointed and qualified him/her to preach the Gospel to the meek, the poor, the wealthy, the afflicted. You have sent _____ to bind up and heal the brokenhearted, to proclaim liberty to the physical and spiritual captives, and the opening of the prison and of the eyes to those who are bound.

_____ shall be called the priest of the Lord. People will speak of him/her as a minister of God. He/she shall eat the wealth of the nations.

We pray and believe that no weapon that is formed against _____ shall prosper and that any tongue that rises against him/her in judgment shall be shown to be in the wrong. We pray that You prosper _____ abundantly, Lord—physically, spiritually and financially.

We confess that _____ holds fast and follows the pattern of wholesome and sound teaching in all faith and love which is for us in Christ Jesus. _____ guards and keeps with the greatest love the precious and excellently adapted Truth, which has been entrusted to him/her by the Holy Spirit, Who makes His home in _____.

Lord, we pray and believe that each and every day freedom of utterance is given _____, that he/she will open his/her mouth boldly and coura-geously as he/she ought to do to get the Gospel to the people. Thank You, Lord, for the added strength which comes superhumanly that You have given him/her.

We hereby confess that we shall stand behind _____ and undergird him/her in prayer. We will say only that good thing that will edify _____. We will not allow ourselves to judge him/her, but will continue to intercede for him/her and speak and pray blessings upon him/her in the name of Jesus. Thank You, Jesus, for the answers. Hallelujah!

Scripture References

Isaiah 11:2,3   2 Timothy 1:13,14

Isaiah 61:1,6   Ephesians 6:19,20

Isaiah 54:17   1 Peter 3:12

28

Missionaries

*F*ather, we lift before You those in the Body of Christ who are out in the field carrying the good news of the Gospel—not only in this country but also around the world. We lift those in the Body of Christ who are suffering persecution—those who are in prison for their beliefs. Father, we know that You watch over Your Word to perform it, that Your Word prospers in the thing for which You sent it. Therefore, we speak Your Word and establish Your covenant on this earth. We pray here, and others receive the answer there by the Holy Spirit.

Thank You, Father, for revealing unto Your people the integrity of Your Word and that they must be firm in faith against the devil's onset, withstanding him. Father, You are their light, salvation, refuge and stronghold. You hide them in Your shelter and set them high upon a rock. It is Your will that each one prospers, is in good health and lives in victory. You set the prisoners free, feed the hungry, execute justice, rescue and deliver.

We commission the ministering spirits to go forth and provide the necessary help for and assistance to these heirs of salvation. We and they are strong in the Lord and in the power of Your might, quenching every dart of the devil in Jesus' name.

Father, we use our faith, covering these in the Body of Christ with Your Word. We say that no weapon formed against them shall prosper, and any tongue that rises against them in judgment they shall show to be in the wrong. This peace, security and triumph over opposition is their inheritance as Your children. This is the righteousness which they obtain from You, Father, which You impart to them as their justification. They are far from even the thought of destruction, for they shall not fear, and terror shall not come near them.

Father, You say You will establish them to the end—keep them steadfast, give them strength and guarantee their vindication; that is, be their warrant against all accusation or indictment. They are not anxious beforehand how they shall reply in defense or what they are to say, for the Holy Spirit teaches them in that very hour and moment what they ought to say to those in the outside world, their speech being seasoned with salt.

We commit these our brothers and sisters in the Lord to You, Father, deposited into Your charge, entrusting them to Your protection and care, for You are faithful. You strengthen them and set them on a firm foundation and guard them from the evil one. We join our voices in praise unto You, Most High, that You might silence the enemy and avenger. Praise the Lord! Greater is He Who is in us than he who is in the world!

Scripture References

Jeremiah 1:12	*Ephesians 6:10,16*
Isaiah 55:11	*Isaiah 54:14,17*
1 Peter 5:9	*1 Corinthians 1:8*
Psalm 27:1,5	*Luke 12:11,12*
3 John 2	*Colossians 4:6*
1 John 5:4,5	*Acts 20:32*

Psalm 146:7

Psalm 144:7

Matthew 18:18

Hebrews 1:14

2 Thessalonians 3:3

Psalm 8:2

1 John 4:4

29

Prosperity for Ministering Servants

*F*ather, how we praise You and thank You for Your Word, knowing that You watch over Your Word to perform it, and no Word of Yours returns void, but accomplishes that which You please, and it prospers in the thing for which You sent it.

Father, in the name of Jesus, we pray, and believe that those in Your Body who have sown the seed of spiritual good among the people reap from the people's material benefits, for You directed that those who publish the good news of the Gospel should live and get their maintenance by the Gospel.

The people's gifts are the fragrant odor of an offering and sacrifice which You, Father, welcome and in which You delight. You will liberally supply, fill to the full, the people's every need according to Your riches in glory in Christ Jesus.

Father, it is your will that those who receive instruction in the Word of God share all good things with their teachers, contributing to their support. We confess that Your people will not lose heart and grow weary and faint in acting nobly and doing right, for in due time and at the appointed season they shall reap, if they do not loosen and relax their courage and faint.

So then, as occasion and opportunity are open to the people, they do good to all people, not only being useful and profitable to them, but also doing what is for their spiritual good and advantage.

We pray that your people will be a blessing, especially to those of the household of faith—those who belong to God's family. Help us to remember that whoever sows generously will also reap generously.

God, You are then able to make all grace, every favor and earthly blessing, come to Your people in abundance, so that they are always and under all circumstances possessing enough to require no aid or support and furnished in abundance for every good work and charitable donation.

As Your people give, their deeds of justice and goodness and kindness and benevolence go on and endure forever. And God, You provide the seed for the sower and bread for the eating, so You also will provide and multiply the people's resources for sowing and increase the fruits of their righteousness. Thus Your people are enriched in all things and in every way so that they can be generous, and their generosity, as it is administered by Your teachers, will bring thanksgiving to God.

As it is written, **Give, and it shall be given unto you; good measure, pressed down, and shaken together, and running over, shall men give into your bosom** (Luke 6:38). Praise the Lord!

Scripture References

Jeremiah 1:12   Galatians 6:6-10

Isaiah 55:11   2 Corinthians 9:6-11

1 Corinthians 9:11-14   Luke 6:38

Philippians 4:17-19

30

Success of a Meeting

*F*ather, in the name of Jesus, we approach the throne of grace boldly and confidently. May the Word of God come forth accurately and in love during the _____ meeting.

We ask You anoint each speaker to teach and preach the Word of God in simplicity, with boldness and with accuracy during the entire meeting. We ask that those who hear will not be able to resist the wisdom and the inspiration of the Holy Spirit that will be spoken through your ministers of the Gospel.

As Your Word is taught we ask You to cause people to open their spiritual eyes and ears that they might turn from darkness to light—from the power of Satan to You, Father, and they will personally confess Jesus as their Lord.

We commit this meeting to You, Father; we deposit it into Your charge—entrusting this meeting, the people who will hear and the people who will speak into Your protection and care. We commend this meeting to the Word—the commands and counsels and promises of Your unmerited favor. Father, we know Your Word will build up the people and cause them to realize that they are joint-heirs with Jesus.

We believe, Father, that as Your Word comes forth, an anointing will be upon the speaker and _____ *(name)* will be submitted completely to the Holy Spirit, for the Word of God that is spoken is alive and full of power, making it active, operative, energizing, and effective, being sharper than any two-edged sword. We ask You to meet the need of every person spiritually, physically, mentally and financially.

We thank You, Father, and praise You that, because we have asked and agreed together, these petitions have come to pass. Let these words with which we have made supplication before the Lord be near to the Lord our God day and night, that He may maintain the cause and right of His people in the _____ (meeting) as each day of it requires! We believe that all the earth's people will know that the Lord is God and there is no other! Hallelujah!

Scripture References

James 5:16	*Acts 26:18*
Matthew 18:19	*Acts 20:32*
Ephesians 6:19	*Hebrews 4:12*
Acts 6:10	*Philippians 4:19*
Ephesians 1:18	*1 Kings 8:59,60*

Prayers for the World

31

Salvation of the Lost

*F*ather, it is written in Your Word, **First of all, then, I admonish and urge that petitions, prayers, intercessions and thanksgivings be offered on behalf of all men** (1 Timothy 2:1 AMP).

Therefore, Father, we bring the lost of the world this day—every man, woman and child from here to the farthest corner of the earth—before You. As we intercede, we use our faith, believing that thousands this day have the opportunity to make Jesus their Lord.

For everyone who has that opportunity, Satan, we bind your blinding spirit of antichrist and loose you from your assignment against those who have that opportunity to make Jesus Lord.

We ask the Lord of the harvest to thrust the perfect laborers across these lives this day to share the good news of the Gospel in a special way so that they will listen and understand it. We believe that they will not be able to resist the wooing of the Holy Spirit, for You, Father, bring them to repentance by Your goodness and love.

We confess that they who have never been told of Jesus shall see. They who have never heard of Jesus shall understand. And they shall come out of the snare of the devil, who has held them captive. They shall open their eyes and turn from darkness to light—from the power of Satan to You, God!

Scripture References

1 Timothy 2:1,2 AMP	*Romans 2:4*
Matthew 18:18	*Romans 15:21*
Matthew 9:38	*2 Timothy 2:26*

32

Nations and Continents

*F*ather, Jesus is our Salvation. He is the God-revealing light to the non-Jewish nations, and of glory for your people Israel. As members of the Body of Christ we are asking You to give us the nations for our inheritance, and the ends of the earth for our possession. All kings shall fall down before You, all nations shall serve You. In the name of Jesus, we bring before You the nation (or continent) of _____ and her leaders. We ask You to rebuke leaders for our sakes so that we may live a quiet and peaceable life in all godliness and honesty.

We pray that skillful and godly wisdom will enter the heart of _____'s leaders and that knowledge shall be pleasant to them, that discretion will watch over them and understanding will keep them and deliver them from the way of evil and from the evil men.

We pray that the upright shall dwell in the government(s)—that men and women of integrity, blameless and complete in Your sight, Father, shall remain, but the wicked shall be cut off and the treacherous shall be rooted out. We pray that those in authority winnow the wicked from among the good and bring the threshing wheel over them to separate the chaff from the grain, for loving-kindness and mercy, truth and faithfulness preserve those in authority and their offices are upheld by the people's loyalty.

We confess and believe that the decisions made by the leaders are divinely directed by You, Father, and their mouths should not transgress in judgment. Therefore, the leaders are men and women of discernment, understanding and knowledge so the stability of _____ will long continue. We pray that the uncompromisingly righteous be in authority in _____ so that the people there can rejoice.

Father, it is an abomination for leaders to commit wickedness. We pray that their offices be established and made secure by righteousness and that right and just lips are a delight to those in authority and that they love those who speak what is right.

We pray and believe that the good news of the Gospel is published in this land. We thank You for laborers of the harvest to publish Your Word that Jesus is Lord in _____. We thank You for raising up intercessors to pray for _____ in Jesus' name. Amen.

Scripture References

1 Timothy 2:1,2	Proverbs 28:2
Psalm 105:14	Proverbs 29:2
Proverbs 2:10-15	Acts 12:24
Proverbs 2:21,22	Psalm 68:11
Proverbs 20:26,28	Luke 2:31 THE MESSAGE
Proverbs 21:1	Psalms 2:8
Proverbs 16:10,12,13	Psalms 72:11

Here is a list of continents and nations to help you as you pray for the world:

Continents:

Africa	North America
Asia	Oceania
Europe	South America

Nations:

Afghanistan	Austria
Albania	Azerbaijan
Algeria	Bahamas
Andorra	Bahrain
Angola	Bangladesh
Antigua and Barbuda	Barbados
Argentina	Belarus
Armenia	Belgium
Australia	Belize

Benin

Bhutan

Bolivia

Bosnia-Hercegovina

Botswana

Brazil

Brunei

Bulgaria

Burkina Faso

Burma

Burundi

Cambodia

Cameroon

Canada

Cape Verde

Central African Republic

Chad

Chile

China, People's Republic of

Colombia

Comoros

Congo

Costa Rica

Cote D'Ivoire (Ivory Coast)

Croatia

Cuba

Cyprus

Czech Republic

Denmark

Djibouti

Dominica

Dominican Republic

Ecuador

Egypt

El Salvador

Equatorial Guinea	Guyana
Eritrea	Haiti
Estonia	Honduras
Ethiopia	Hungary
Fiji	Iceland
Finland	India
France	Indonesia
Gabon	Iran
The Gambia	Iraq
Georgia	Ireland
Germany	Israel
Ghana	Italy
Greece	Jamaica
Grenada	Japan
Guatemala	Jordan
Guinea	Kazakstan
Guinea-Bissau	Kenya

Kiribati	Malaysia
North Korea	Maldives
South Korea	Mali
Kuwait	Malta
Kyrgyzstan	Marshall Islands
Laos	Mauritania
Latvia	Mauritius
Lebanon	Mexico
Lesotho	Micronesia
Liberia	Moldova
Libya	Monaco
Liechtenstein	Mongolia
Lithuania	Morocco
Luxembourg	Mozambique
Macedonia	Namibia
Madagascar	Nauru
Malawi	Nepal

Netherlands

New Zealand

Nicaragua

Niger

Nigeria

Norway

Oman

Pakistan

Palau

Panama

Papua New Guinea

Paraguay

Peru

Philippines

Poland

Portugal

Qatar

Romania

Russia

Rwanda

St. Kitts & Nevis

St. Lucia

St. Vincent &
  The Grenadines

San Marino

Sáo Tomé E Príncipe

Saudi Arabia

Senegal

Seychelles

Sierra Leone

Singapore

Slovakia

Slovenia

Solomon Islands

Somalia

South Africa	Turkmenistan
Spain	Tuvalu
Sri Lanka	Uganda
Sudan	Ukraine
Suriname	United Arab Emirates
Swaziland	United Kingdom
Sweden	United States of America
Switzerland	Uruguay
Syria	Uzbekistan
Taiwan	Vanuatu
Tajikistan	Vatican City State
Tanzania	Venezuela
Thailand	Vietnam
Togo	Western Samoa
Tonga	Yemen
Trinidad & Tobago	Zaïre
Tunisia	Zambia
Turkey	Zimbabwe

33

Peace of Jerusalem

*F*ather, in the name of Jesus and according to your Word, I long and pray for the peace of Jerusalem, that its inhabitants may be born again. I pray that You, Lord, will be a refuge and a stronghold to the children of Israel. Father, Your Word says "multitudes, multitudes are in the valley of decision" and whoever calls upon Your name shall be delivered and saved.

Have mercy upon Israel and be gracious to them, O Lord, and consider that they fight for their land to be restored. You, Lord, are their strength and stronghold in their day of trouble. We pray that they are righteous before You and that You will make even their enemies to be at peace with them. Your Word says You will deliver those for whom we intercede, who are not innocent, through the cleanness of our hands. May they realize that their defense and shield depend on You.

We thank You for Your Word, Lord, that You have a covenant with Israel and that You will take away their sin. They are Your beloved. Your Word also says that Your gifts are irrevocable, that You never withdraw them once they are given, and that You do not change your mind about those to whom You give Your grace or to whom You send Your call. Though they have been disobedient and rebellious toward You, Lord, we pray that now they will repent and obtain Your mercy and forgiveness through Your Son, Jesus. We praise You, Lord, for Your compassion and Your forgiveness to Your people. We praise You that they are under Your protection and divine guidance, that they are Your special possession, Your peculiar treasure, and that You will spare them, for we have read in Your Word that all Israel shall be saved!

Thank You, Father, for delivering us all from every evil work and the authority You have given us with the name of Jesus. We love You and praise You. Every day, with its new reasons, do we praise You!

I commit to pray for the peace of Jerusalem! May they prosper that love you in "the Holy City!" Peace be within your walls and prosperity within your palaces!

Scripture References

Joel 3:14	Romans 11:29
Job 22:30 AMP	Isaiah 45:17

Prayers for
Those in Authority

34

American Government

*F*ather, in Jesus' name, we give thanks for the United States and its government. We hold up in prayer before You the men and women who are in positions of authority. We pray and intercede for the president, the representatives, the senators, the judges of our land, the policemen and the policewomen, as well as the governors and mayors, and for all those who are in authority over us in any way. We pray that the Spirit of the Lord rests upon them.

We believe that skillful and godly wisdom has entered into the heart of our president and knowledge is pleasant to him. Discretion watches over him; understanding keeps him and delivers him from the way of evil and from evil men.

Father, we ask that You compass the president about with men and women who make their hearts and ears attentive to godly counsel and do that which is right in Your sight. We believe You cause them to be men and women of integrity who are obedient concerning us, that we may lead quiet and peaceable lives in all godliness and honesty. We pray that the upright shall dwell in our government—that men and women blameless and complete in Your sight, Father, shall remain in these positions of authority but that the wicked shall be cut off from our government and the treacherous shall be rooted out of it.

Your Word declares, **Blessed is the nation whose God is the Lord** (Ps. 33:12). We receive Your blessing. Father, You are our refuge and stronghold in times of trouble (high cost, destitution and desperation). So we declare with our mouths that Your people dwell safely in this land, and we *prosper* abundantly. We are more than conquerors through Christ Jesus!

It is written in Your Word that the heart of the king is in the hand of the Lord, and you turn it whichever way You desire. We believe the heart of our leader is in Your hand and that his decisions are divinely directed of the Lord.

We give thanks unto You that the good news of the Gospel is published in our land. The Word of the

Lord prevails and grows mightily in the hearts and lives of the people. We give thanks for this land and the leaders You have given to us, in Jesus' name.

Jesus is Lord over the United States!

Scripture References

1 Timothy 2:1-3	*Deuteronomy 28:10,11*
Proverbs 2:10-12,21,22	*Romans 8:37*
Psalm 33:12	*Proverbs 21:1*
Psalm 9:9	*Acts 12:24*

35

School Systems and Children

*F*ather, we thank You that the entrance of Your Word brings light and thank You that You watch over Your Word to perform it. Father, we bring before You the _____ school system(s) and the men and women who are in positions of authority within the school system(s).

We ask You to give them skillful and godly wisdom; that Your knowledge might be pleasant to them. Then, discretion will watch over them; understanding will keep them and deliver them from the way of evil and from evil men. We pray that men and women of integrity—blameless and complete in Your sight—remain in these positions but that the wicked be cut off and the treacherous be rooted out, in the name of Jesus. Father, we thank You for born-again, Spirit-filled people in these positions.

Father, we bring our children, our young people, before You. We speak forth Your Word boldly and confidently, Father, that we and our households are saved in the name of Jesus. We are redeemed from the curse of the law, for Jesus was made a curse for us. *Our sons and daughters are not given to another people.* We enjoy our children, and they shall not go into captivity, in the name of Jesus.

As parents, we train our children in the way they should go, and when they are old they shall not depart from it.

Our children shrink from whatever might offend You, Father, and discredit the name of Christ. They show themselves to be blameless, guileless, innocent and uncontaminated children of God without blemish (faultless, unrebukable) in the midst of a crooked and wicked generation, holding out to it and offering to all the Word of Life. Thank You, Father, that You give them knowledge and skill in all learning and wisdom, and bring them into favor with those around them.

Father, we pray and intercede that these young people, their parents and the leaders in the school system(s) separate themselves from contact with contaminating and corrupting influences. They cleanse themselves from everything that would contaminate and defile their spirits, souls and bodies. We confess that they shun immorality and all sexual looseness— flee from impurity in thought, word or deed. They live and conduct themselves honorably and becomingly, as in the open light of day. We confess and believe that they shun youthful lusts and flee from them, in the name of Jesus.

Father we ask you to commission the ministering spirits to go forth and police the area, dispelling the forces of darkness.

Father, we thank You that in Christ all the treasures of divine wisdom (of comprehensive insight into the ways and purposes of God) and all the riches of spiritual knowledge and enlightenment are stored up and lie hidden for us, and we walk in Him.

We praise You, Father, that we shall see _____ walking in the ways of piety and virtue, revering Your name, Father. Those who err in spirit will come to understanding and those who murmur discontentedly will accept instruction in the way, Jesus, to Your will and carry out Your purposes in their lives, for You, Father, occupy first place in their hearts. We surround _____ with our faith.

Thank you, Father, that You are the delivering God. Thank You, that the good news of the Gospel is published throughout our school system(s). Thank You for intercessors to stand on Your Word and for laborers of the harvest to preach Your Word in Jesus' name. Praise the Lord!

Scripture References

Psalm 119:130	2 Timothy 2:21
Jeremiah 1:12	Corinthians 7:1
Proverbs 2:10-12	1 Corinthians 6:18
Proverbs 2:21,22	Romans 13:13
Acts 16:31	Ephesians 5:4
Galatians 3:13	2 Timothy 2:22
Deuteronomy 28:32,41	Matthew 18:18

Proverbs 22:6

Philippians 2:15,16

Daniel 1:17

Daniel 1:9

1 John 2:17

2 Timothy 2:26

Hebrews 1:14

Colossians 2:3

Isaiah 29:23,24

Prayers for the Needs of Others

36

Salvation

*F*ather, in the name of Jesus, we come before You in prayer and in faith, believing. It is written in Your Word that Jesus came to save the lost. You wish all men to be saved and to know Your Divine Truth; therefore, Father, we bring _____ before You this day.

Satan, we bind you in the name of Jesus and loose you from the activities in _____'s life!

Father, we ask the Lord of the harvest to thrust the perfect laborer into his/her path, a laborer to share Your Gospel in a special way so that he/she will listen and understand it. As Your laborer ministers to him/her, we believe that he/she will come to his/her senses —come out of the snare of the devil, who has held him/her captive, and make Jesus the Lord of his/her life.

Your Word says that You will deliver those for whom we intercede, who are not innocent, through the cleanness *of our hands*. We're standing on Your

Word, and from this moment on, Father, we shall praise You and thank You for his/her salvation. We have committed this matter into Your hands, and with our faith we see _____ saved, filled with Your Spirit, with a full and clear knowledge of Your Word. Amen—so be it!

Each day after praying this prayer, thank the Lord for this person's salvation. Rejoice and praise God for the victory! Confess the above prayer as done! Thank Him for sending the laborer. Thank Him that Satan is bound. Hallelujah!

Scripture References

Luke 19:10   2 Timothy 2:26

Matthew 18:18   Job 22:30

Matthew 9:38

37

Spirit-Controlled Life

*F*ather, I pray for all saints everywhere. Help us remain teachable that we may receive instruction from the apostles, prophets, evangelists, pastors and teachers. We will be Your children equipped for the work of ministry, for the edifying of the body of Christ. Bring us to the unity of the faith and of the knowledge of the Son of God, to a perfect man, to the measure of the stature of the fullness of Christ.

Father, there is now no condemnation to those who walk according to the Spirit, because through Christ Jesus the law of the Spirit of life set us free from the law of sin and death.

Grant us the grace to live the life of the Spirit. Father, You condemned sin in the flesh [subdued, overcame, deprived it of its power over us. Now the righteous and just requirement of the Law is fully met in us who live and move in the ways of the Spirit [our lives governed and controlled by the Holy Spirit].

We purpose to live our lives according to the Spirit and we are controlled by the desires of the Spirit. We set our minds on and seek those things, which gratify the Holy Spirit. We no longer live the life of the flesh; we live the life of the Spirit. The Holy Spirit of God really dwells within us, directing and controlling us.

On the authority of Your word we declare that we are more than conquerors and are gaining a surpassing victory through Jesus who loves us. We refuse to let ourselves be overcome with evil, but overcome and master evil with good. We have on the full armor of light, clothed with the Lord Jesus Christ, the Messiah, and make no provision for indulging the flesh.

May we always be doers of God's Word. We have God's wisdom, and we draw it forth with prayer. We are peace-loving, full of compassion and good fruits. We are free from doubts, wavering, and insincerity. We are subject to God, our Father.

We are strong in the Lord and the power of His might. Therefore, we take our stand against the devil, and resist him; he flees from us. We draw close to God and God draws close to us. We do not fear for God never leaves us.

In Christ, we are filled with the Godhead: Father, Son and Holy Spirit. Jesus is our Lord!

Scripture References

Romans 8:2,4,9,14,31,37

James 3:17

Romans 12:21

Hebrews 13:5

Romans 13:12,14

James 4:7,8

James 1:22

Colossians 2:10

38

Renew Fellowship

*F*ather, You hasten Your Word to perform it. I believe that _____ is a disciple of Christ, taught of You, Lord, and obedient to Your will. Great is his/her peace and undisturbed composure. _____ has You in person for his/her teacher. He/she has listened and learned from You and has come to Jesus.

_____ continues to hold to things he/she has learned and of which he/she is convinced. From childhood he/she has had knowledge of and been acquainted with the Word, which is able to instruct him/her and give him/her the understanding of the salvation which comes through faith in Christ Jesus. Father, You will heal _____, lead _____, recompense _____ and restore comfort to _____.

Jesus gives _____ eternal life. He/she shall never lose it or perish throughout the ages, to all eternity. _____ shall never by any means be destroyed. You, Father, have given _____ to Jesus. You are greater and mightier than all else; no one is able to snatch _____ out of Your hand.

I pray and believe that _____ comes to his/her senses and escapes out of the snare of the devil, who has held him/her captive, and that _____ would judge himself/herself.

_____ has become a fellow-heir with Christ, the Messiah, and shares in all He has for him/her and holds the first newborn confidence and original assured expectation firm and unshaken to the end. _____ casts not away his/her confidence, for it has great recompense of reward.

Thank You for giving _____ wisdom and revelation—quickening him/her to Your Word. Thank You that _____ enjoys fellowship with You and Jesus and with fellow believers.

Scripture References

Jeremiah 1:12

John 6:45

Isaiah 54:13

2 Timothy 3:14,15

Isaiah 57:18

John 10:28,29

1 John 5:16

2 Timothy 2:26

1 Corinthians 11:31

Matthew 18:18

Hebrews 3:14

Hebrews 10:35

Ephesians 1:17

1 John 1:3

39

Deliverance From Satan and His Demonic Forces

If the person for whom you are interceding has not confessed Jesus as Savior and Lord, pray specifically for his/her salvation, if you have not already done so. Stand and thank the Father that it is done in the name of Jesus. Then pray:

Father, in the name of Jesus, I come boldly to Your throne of grace and present _____ before You. I stand in the gap and intercede in behalf of _____, knowing that the Holy Spirit within me takes hold together with me against the evils that would attempt to hold _____ in bondage. I unwrap _____ from the bonds of wickedness with my prayers and take my shield of faith and quench every fiery dart of the adversary that would come against _____.

Father, You say that whatever I bind on earth is bound in heaven, and whatever I loose on earth is loosed in heaven. You say for me to cast out demons in the name of Jesus.

*In the name of Jesus I bind _____'s body, soul and spirit to the will and purposes of God for his/her life. I bind _____'s mind, will and emotions to the will of God. I bind him/her to the truth and to the blood of Jesus. I bind his/her mind to the mind of Christ that the very thoughts, feelings and purposes of His heart would be within his/her thoughts.

I loose every old, wrong, ungodly pattern of thinking, attitude, idea, desire, belief, motivation, habit and behavior from him/her. I tear down, crush, smash and destroy every stronghold associated with these things. I loose any stronghold in his/her life that has been justifying and protecting hard feelings against anyone. I loose the stronghold of unforgiveness, fear and distrust from him/her. I bind and loose these things in Jesus name.

* *Shattering Your Strongholds,* Copyright ©1992 by Liberty Savard, Bridge-Logos Publishers, North Brunswick, NJ (pg. 171-172)

Ministering spirits of God, you go forth in the name of Jesus and provide the necessary help to and assistance for _____.

Father, I have laid hold of _____'s salvation and his/her confession of the Lordship of Jesus Christ. I speak of things that are not as though they were, for I choose to look at the unseen—the eternal things of God. I say that Satan shall not get an advantage over _____, for I am not ignorant of Satan's devices. I resist Satan, and he has run in terror from _____ in the name of Jesus. I give Satan no place in _____. I plead the blood of the Lamb over _____, for Satan and his cohorts are overcome by that blood and Your Word. I thank You, Father, that I tread on serpents and scorpions and over all the power of the enemy in _____'s behalf. _____ is delivered from this present evil world. He/she is delivered from the powers of darkness and translated into the Kingdom of Your dear Son!

Father, I ask You now to fill those vacant places within _____ with Your redemption, Your Word, Your Holy Spirit, Your love, Your wisdom,

Your righteousness and Your revelation knowledge, in the name of Jesus.

I thank You, Father, that _____ is redeemed by the blood of Jesus out of the hand of Satan. He/she is justified and made righteous by the blood of Jesus and belongs to You—spirit, soul and body. I thank You that every enslaving yoke is broken, for he/she will not become the slave of anything or be brought under its power, in the name of Jesus. _____ has escaped the snare of the devil, who has held him/her captive, and henceforth does Your will, Father, which is to glorify You in his/her spirit, soul and body.

Thank You, Father, that Jesus was manifested that He might destroy the works of the devil. Satan's works are destroyed in _____'s life in the name of Jesus. Hallelujah! _____ walks in the Kingdom of God, which is righteousness, peace and joy in the Holy Spirit! Praise the Lord! Amen.

Once this prayer has been prayed, thank the Father that Satan and his cohorts are bound. Stand firm, fixed, immovable and steadfast on your confessions of faith as you intercede on this person's behalf, for **greater is He that is in you, than he that is in the world** (1 John 4:4).

Scripture References

Hebrews 4:16	*2 Corinthians 2:11*
Ezekiel 22:30	*James 4:7*
Romans 8:26	*Ephesians 4:27*
Isaiah 58:6	*Revelation 12:11*
Ephesians 6:16	*Luke 10:19*
Matthew 18:18	*Galatians 1:4*
Mark 16:17	*Colossians 1:13*
Ephesians 6:12	*Matthew 12:43-45*
Colossians 2:15	*1 Corinthians 6:12*
Matthew 12:29	*2 Timothy 2:26*
Hebrews 1:14	*1 John 3:8*
Romans 4:17	*Romans 14:17*
2 Corinthians 4:18	

40

Employment

*F*ather, in Jesus' name, we believe and confess Your Word over _____ today, knowing that You watch over Your Word to perform it. Your Word prospers in _____ whereto it is sent! Father, You are his/her source of every consolation, comfort and encouragement. _____ is courageous and grows in strength.

His/her desire is to owe no man anything but to love him. Therefore, _____ is strong and lets not his/her hands be weak or slack, for his/her work shall be rewarded. His/her wages are not counted as a favor or a gift, but as something owed to him/her. _____ makes it his/her ambition and definitely endeavors to live quietly and peacefully, minds his/her own affairs and works with his/her hands. He/she is correct and honorable and commands the respect of the outside world, being self-supporting, dependent on nobody and having need of nothing, for You, Father, supply to the full his/her every need.

He/she works in quietness and earns his/her own food and other necessities. He/she is not weary of doing right and continues in well-doing without weakening. _____ learns to apply himself/herself to good deeds—to honest labor and honorable employment—so that he/she is able to meet necessary demands whenever the occasion may require.

Father, You know the record of his/her works and what he/she is doing. You have set before _____ a door wide open which no one is able to shut.

_____ does not fear and is not dismayed, for You, Father, strengthen him/her. You, Father, help _____ in Jesus' name, for in Jesus _____ has perfect peace and confidence and is of good cheer, for Jesus overcame the world and deprived it of its power to harm _____. He/she does not fret or have anxiety about anything, for Your peace, Father, mounts guard over his/her heart and mind. _____ knows the secret of facing every situation, for he/she is self-sufficient in Christ's sufficiency.

_____ guards his/her mouth and tongue, keeping himself/herself from trouble.

_____ prizes Your wisdom, Father, and acknowledges You. You direct—make straight and plain—his/her path, and You promote him/her. Therefore, Father, _____ increases in Your wisdom (in broad and full understanding) and in stature and years and in favor with You, Father, and with man!

Scripture References

Jeremiah 1:12	Titus 3:14
Isaiah 55:11	Revelation 3:8
2 Corinthians 1:3	Isaiah 41:10
1 Corinthians 16:13	John 16:33
Romans 13:8	Philippians 4:6,7
2 Chronicles 15:7	Philippians 4:12,13
Romans 4:4	Proverbs 21:23
1 Thessalonians 4:11,12	Proverbs 3:6
2 Thessalonians 3:12,13	Proverbs 4:8
Luke 2:52	

41

Finding Favor With Others

*F*ather, in the name of Jesus, You make Your face to shine upon and enlighten _____ and are gracious (kind, merciful and giving favor) to him/her. _____ is the head and not the tail. _____ is above only and not beneath.

Thank You for favor for _____, who seeks Your Kingdom and Your righteousness and diligently seeks good. _____ is a blessing to You, Lord, and is a blessing to _____ *(name them: family, neighbors, business associates, etc.).* Grace (favor) is with _____ , who loves the Lord Jesus in sincerity. _____ extends favor, honor and love to _____ *(names).* _____ is flowing in Your Love, Father. You are pouring out upon _____ the spirit of favor. You crown him/her with glory and honor, for he/she is Your child—Your workmanship.

_____ is a success today. _____ is someone very special with You, Lord. _____ is growing in the Lord—waxing strong in spirit. Father, You give _____ knowledge and skill in all learning and wisdom.

You bring _____ to find favor, compassion, and loving-kindness with _____ *(names)*. _____ obtains favor in the sight of all who look upon him/her this day in the name of Jesus. _____ is filled with Your fullness—rooted and grounded in love. You are doing exceeding abundantly above all that _____ asks or thinks, for Your mighty power is taking over in _____.

Thank You, Father, that _____ is well-favored by You and by man, in Jesus' name!

Scripture References

Numbers 6:25	*Psalm 8:5*
Deuteronomy 28:13	*Ephesians 2:10*

Matthew 6:33	*Luke 2:40*
Proverbs 11:27	*Daniel 1:17*
Ephesians 6:24	*Daniel 1:9*
Luke 6:38	*Esther 2:15,17*
Zechariah 12:10	*Ephesians 3:19,20*

42

Improving Communication

_____ is a disciple of Christ—taught of the Lord and obedient to His will. Great is his/her peace and undisturbed composure. _____ is constantly renewed in the spirit of his/her mind—having a fresh mental and spiritual attitude—and is putting on the new nature—the regenerate self—created in God's image, God-like in true righteousness and holiness.

His/her life lovingly expresses truth in all things—speaking truly, dealing truly, living truly. _____ is enfolded in love, growing up in every way and in all things into Him Who is the Head, even Christ, the Messiah, the Anointed One. His/her mouth shall utter truth. _____ speaks excellent and princely things—the opening of his/her lips is for right things.

All the words of his/her mouth are righteous. There is nothing contrary to truth or crooked in them.

_____ inclines his/her heart to Your testimonies, Father, and not to covetousness (robbery, sensuality or unworthy riches). _____ does not love or cherish the world. The love of the Father is in him/her. _____ is set free from the lust of the flesh (craving for sensual gratification), the lust of the eyes (greedy longings of the mind) and the pride of life (assurance in his/her own resources or in the stability of earthly things). _____ perceives and knows the truth and that nothing false is of the truth.

_____ prizes Your wisdom, Father, and exalts it, and it will exalt and promote him/her. _____ attends to God's words, consents and submits to Your sayings. _____ keeps them in the center of his/her heart. For they are life to _____ and medicine to all his/her flesh. _____ keeps his/her heart with all diligence, for out of it flow the springs of life.

_____ will do nothing from factional motives through contentiousness, strife, selfishness or for unworthy ends—or prompted by conceit and empty arrogance. Instead, in the true spirit of humility, _____ does regard others as better than himself/herself. _____ esteems and looks upon and is concerned for not merely his/her own interests, but also for the interests of others.

_____ lets this same attitude and purpose and humble mind be in him/her which was in Christ Jesus. Thank You, Father, in Jesus' name.

Scripture References

Isaiah 54:13	Psalm 119:36
Ephesians 4:23,24	1 John 2:15,16,21
Ephesians 4:15	Proverbs 4:8,20-23
Proverbs 8:6-8	Philippians 2:2

43

Peace in a Troubled Marriage

*F*ather, in the name of Jesus, we bring _____ before You. We pray and confess Your Word over them, and as we do, we use our faith, believing that Your Word will come to pass.

Therefore we pray that _____ will let all bitterness, indignation, wrath, passion, rage, bad temper, resentment, brawling, clamor, contention, slander, abuse, evil speaking or blasphemous language be banished from them; also all malice, spite, ill will or baseness of any kind. We pray that _____ have become useful and helpful and kind to each other, tenderhearted, compassionate, understanding, loving-hearted, forgiving one another readily and freely as You, Father, in Christ, forgave them.

Therefore, _____ will be imitators of You, God. They will copy You and follow Your example as well-beloved children imitate their father. _____ will walk in love, esteeming and delighting in one another as Christ loved them and gave Himself up for them as a slain offering and sacrifice to You, God, so that it became a sweet fragrance.

Father, we thank You that _____ will be constantly renewed in the spirit of their minds, having a fresh mental and spiritual attitude. They have put on the new nature and are created in God's image in true righteousness and holiness. They have come to their senses and escaped out of the snare of the devil, who has held them captive, and henceforth will do Your will, which is that they love one another with the God kind of love, united in total peace and harmony and happiness.

Thank You for the answer, Lord. We know it is done now in the name of Jesus.

Scripture References

Ephesians 4:31,32	*Ephesians 4:23,24*
Ephesians 5:1,2	*2 Timothy 2:26*
Matthew 18:18	

PRAYERS THAT AVAIL MUCH *Volume One*

44

Single Believer

_____ is united to the Lord and has become one spirit with Him. _____ shuns immorality and all sexual looseness. _____ flees from impurity in thought, word or deed.

_____ will not sin against his/her body by committing sexual immorality. His/her body is the temple of the Holy Spirit, Whom he/she has received as a gift from God. _____ is not his/her own. _____ was bought for a price and made God's own. _____ will honor God and bring glory to Him in his/her spirit, soul and body, which are God's.

_____ shuns youthful lusts and flees from them and aims at and pursues righteousness—all that is virtuous and good, right living, conformity to the will of God in thought, word and deed. He/she aims at and pursues faith, love and peace—which is harmony and concord with others—in fellowship with all Christians who call upon the name of the Lord out of a pure heart.

_____ shrinks from whatever might offend You, Father, or discredit the name of Christ. _____ shows himself/herself to be a blameless, guileless, innocent and uncontaminated child of God without blemish (faultless) in the midst of a crooked and wicked generation, among whom _____ is seen as a bright light shining out clearly in the dark world, holding out to it and offering to all the Word of Life. Thank You, Father, that Jesus is Lord.

Scripture References

1 Corinthians 6:17-20   Philippians 2:12,15,16

2 Timothy 2:22

45

Single Female Trusting God for a Mate

*F*ather, in the name of Jesus, I believe that You are providing Your very best for _____ and that the man who will be united with _____ in marriage has awakened to righteousness. Father, as You have rejoiced over Jerusalem, so shall the bridegroom rejoice over _____. Thank You, Father, that he will love _____ as Christ loves the Church. He will nourish, carefully protect and cherish _____.

Father, I believe, because he is Your best, that doubts, wavering and insincerity are not a part of him; but he speaks forth the oracles of God, acknowledging Your full counsel with all wisdom and knowledge. He does not speak or act contrary to the Word. He walks totally in love, esteeming and preferring others higher than himself.

Father, I believe that everything not of You shall be removed from _____'s life. And I thank You for the perfecting of Your Word in her life, that she may be thoroughly furnished unto all good works. Father, I praise You for the performance of Your Word in her behalf.

Scripture References

Isaiah 62:5	James 3:17
Ephesians 5:25	Proverbs 8:8

46

Single Male Trusting God for a Mate

*F*ather, in the name of Jesus, I believe that You are providing a suitable helpmate for _____—Father, according to Your Word, one who will adapt herself to _____, respect, honor, prefer and esteem him, stand firmly by his side, united in spirit and purpose, having the same love and being in full accord and of one harmonious mind and intention.

Father, You say in Your Word that a wise, understanding and prudent wife is from You, and he who finds a true wife finds a good thing and obtains favor of You.

Father, I know that _____ has found favor in Your sight, and I praise You and thank You for Your Word, knowing that You watch over it to perform it.

Scripture References

Ephesians 5:22,33   Proverbs 19:14

Proverbs 18:22   Philippians 2:2

47

Prayer for Those with Special Needs

*F*ather, we come before You boldly and confidently, knowing that You watch over Your Word to perform it. You performed miracles throughout history.

We pray for those with special needs and for their families asking You to quicken them to Your Word – that they may be filled with wisdom and revelation knowledge concerning the integrity of Your Word. We pray for the infilling of the Holy Spirit, divine health, the fruit of the recreated human spirit, the gifts of the Holy Spirit, and deliverance. Jesus, You are the Source of every consolation, comfort, and encouragement and they are to be sanctified spirit, soul and body.

We pray for deliverance to bodies and minds, for You, Lord God, are the help of their countenance and the lifter of those bowed down – the joy of the Lord is their strength and stronghold! We ask You to commission ministering spirits to go forth as they hearken to God's Word to provide the necessary help for and assistance to those for whom we are praying.

Nothing is too hard or impossible for You. All things are possible to us who believe. Let our prayers be set forth as incense before You – a sweet fragrance to You! Praise the Lord!

In the name of Jesus we pray. Amen.

Scripture References

Romans 3:4	Mark 16:17
Mark 11:23,24	Jeremiah 1:12
Psalm 42:11	1 Peter 2:24
Acts 3:16	Psalm 146:8
Matthew 8:17	2 Corinthians 4:4
Nehemiah 8:10	Mark 7:35
John 10:10	Psalm 103:20
Proverbs 20:12	Galatians 3:13

Matthew 9:37,38

Romans 8:2

Psalm 119:89

2 Corinthians 1:3

Matthew 18:18

Mark 9:23

Psalm 127:3

Luke 1:37

Ephesians 1:17,18

Ephesians 2:6

Jeremiah 32:27

1 Thessalonians 5:23

Proverbs 2:21,22

Psalm 141:2

48

Deliverance From Corrupt Companions

Father, in the name of Jesus, I ask You to open the eyes of _____'s understanding that he might not be deceived by the influence of corrupt and depraved people. Thank You for causing him to come alive, and awakening him that he might return to sober sense and his right mind.

Father, I forgive his sins, and come before You asking for mercy—mercy that triumphs over judgement. Thank You for drawing him to yourself with cords and bands of love, and leading him to repentance with Your goodness. Then, he will separate himself from contact with contaminating influences and cleanse himself from everything that would defile his spirit, soul and body.

In the name of Jesus I bind his mind to the mind of Christ that he might live and conduct himself honorably and becomingly as in the open light of the day. I loose him from the wrong thought patterns of his former lifestyle that was controlled by a set of values inspired by the Adversary who misleads those who have not come alive to Christ.

I ask you to give him a willing heart that he might be loyally subject (submissive) to the governing (civil) authority—not resisting nor setting himself up against them. He shall be obedient, prepared, and willing to do any upright and honorable work. He shall walk as a companion with wise men, and he shall be wise.

_____ is pardoned through the name of Jesus and because he confesses his name. He is victorious over the wicked one because he has come to know and recognize and be aware of the Father.

As _____'s mind is renewed by the Word, the Word dwells and remains in him and he dwells in the Son and in the Father always. God's nature abides in _____—his principle of life remains permanently within him and he cannot practice sinning because he is born of God. The law of the Spirit of Life in Christ Jesus has made _____ free from the law of sin and death. Thank You Father, for watching over your Word to perform it in Jesus' name! Amen.

Scripture References

1 Corinthians 15:33,34a	*Proverbs 28:7*
2 Timothy 2:21	*1 Thessalonians 5:22*
2 Corinthians 7:1	*1 John 2:12-16*
Romans 13:13	*1 John 2:21,24*
1 Peter 2:1	*1 John 3:9*
Romans 13:1,2	*Romans 8:2*
Titus 3:1	*Jeremiah 1:12*
Proverbs 13:20	

49

Deliverance From Cults

*F*ather, in the name of Jesus, we come before You in prayer and in faith, believing that Your Word runs swiftly throughout the earth, for the Word of God is not chained or imprisoned. We bring before You _____ *(those, and families of those, involved in cults).*

Father, stretch forth Your hand from above; rescue and deliver _____ out of great waters, from the land of hostile aliens whose mouths speak deceit and whose right hands are raised in taking fraudulent oaths. Their mouths must be stopped, for they are mentally distressing and subverting _____ and whole families by teaching what they ought not teach for the purpose of getting base advantage and disreputable gain. But praise God, they will not get very far, for their rash folly will become obvious to everybody!

Execute justice, precious Father, for the oppressed. Set the prisoners free, open the eyes of the blind, lift up the bowed down, heal the brokenhearted and bind up their wounds. Lift up the humble and downtrodden and cast the wicked down to the ground, in the mighty name of Jesus.

Turn back the hearts of the disobedient, incredulous and unpersuadable to the wisdom of the upright and the knowledge of the will of God, in order to make ready for You, Lord, a people perfectly prepared in spirit, adjusted, disposed and placed in the right moral state.

Father, You say in Your Word to refrain our voices from weeping and our eyes from tears, for our prayers shall be rewarded and _____ shall return from the enemy's land and come again to his/her own country. You will save our offspring from the land of their exile; from the east and the west—sons from afar and daughters from the ends of the earth. We shall see _____ walking in the ways of piety and virtue, revering Your name, Father. Those who err in spirit will come to understanding. Those who murmur discontentedly will accept instruction in the Way, Jesus. Father, You contend with those who contend with us, and You give safety to _____.

*In the name of Jesus I bind _____'s feet to the paths of righteousness that his/her steps would be steady and sure. I bind _____ to the work of the cross with all of its mercy, grace, love, forgiveness and dying to self.

I loose the power and effects of deceptions and lies from him/her. I loose the confusion and blindness of the god of this world from _____'s mind that have kept him/her from seeing the light of the gospel of Jesus Christ. I call forth every precious word of Scripture that has ever entered in his/her mind and heart that it would rise up in power within him/her. I loose the power and effects of any harsh or hard words (word curses) spoken to, about or by _____.

Jesus gave me the keys and the authority to bind and loose these things in His name. Thank you, Lord, for the truth.

* Shattering Your Strongholds, Copyright ©1992 by Liberty Savard, Bridge-Logos Publishers, North Brunswick, NJ (pg. 171-172)

Father we ask you to commission the ministering spirits to go forth and dispel these forces of darkness and bring _____ home in the name of Jesus.

Father, we believe and confess that _____ has had knowledge of and been acquainted with the Word which was able to instruct him/her and give him/her the understanding for salvation, which comes through faith in Christ Jesus. Lord, we pray and believe that You certainly will deliver _____ and draw _____ to yourself from every assault of evil and preserve and bring _____ safe into Your heavenly Kingdom. Glory to You, Father, Who deliver those for whom we intercede in Jesus' name!

Once this prayer has been prayed for an individual, confess it as done. Thank the Father that he or she is delivered, returning from the enemy's land. Thank God that Satan is bound. Thank God for his/her salvation.

Scripture References

Psalm 147:15   Isaiah 43:5,6

2 Timothy 2:9   Isaiah 29:23,24

Psalm 144:7,8   Isaiah 49:25

Titus 1:11

2 Timothy 3:9

Psalm 146:7,8

Psalm 147:3-6

Luke 1:17

Jeremiah 31:16,17

Jeremiah 46:27

Matthew 18:18

2 Timothy 3:2-9

Hebrews 1:14

2 Timothy 3:15

2 Timothy 4:18

Job 22:30

50

Deliverance From Habits

*F*ather, in the name of Jesus and according to Your Word, I believe in my heart and say with my mouth that Jesus is Lord of my life. Since all truth is in Jesus I strip myself of my former nature [put off and discard my old unrenewed self]. I desire to be free from the habit(s) of _____ in the name of Jesus. Father, this habit(s) is not helpful (good for me, expedient and profitable when considered with other things.) I no longer desire to be the slave of wrong habits and behaviors or be brought under their power.

Father, these self-destructive habits are symptoms of a flaw in my soul, my character, and I confess them as sin. I don't want to habitually make the same mistakes over and over. Father, Your Word exposes the wrong thought patterns that are driving me to continue acting out in ways that are contrary to Your

Word. I desire to be continually filled with, and controlled by the Holy Spirit.

Thank you Father for translating me into the kingdom of Your dear Son. Now I am Your garden under cultivation. In the name of Jesus, I throw all spoiled virtue and cancerous evil in the garbage. In simple humility, I purpose to let You, my gardener, landscape me with the Word, making a salvation-garden of my life.

I arm myself with the full armor of God, that armor of a heavily armed soldier which God has supplied for me ...the helmet of salvation...loins girded with truth...feet shod with the preparation of the gospel of peace...the shield of faith...and the Sword of the Sspirit, which is the Word of God. With God's armor on, I am able to stand up against all the strategies and deceits and fiery darts of Satan in the name of Jesus.

Clothed in Your armor I discipline my body and subdue it. With every temptation I choose the way of escape that you provide. Greater is He that is in me than he that is in the world.

Thank You, Lord. I praise You that I am growing spiritually and Your engrafted Word is saving my soul. I strip away the old nature with its habits, and I put on the new man created in Christ Jesus. Hallelujah! Amen.

Scripture References

Romans 10:9,10,13   Hebrews 4:14-16

Matthew 18:18,19   1 John 4:4

1 Corinthians 6:12   Romans 8:4,9

2 Corinthians 10:4,5   Romans 12:21

Ephesians 3:16   Romans 13:14

Ephesians 6:10-17

The Prayers of Jesus

The Prayers of Jesus

Matthew 6:9-13 AMP

Pray, therefore, like this: Our Father Who is in heaven, hallowed (kept holy) be Your name.

Your kingdom come, Your will be done on earth as it is in heaven.

Give us this day our daily bread.

And forgive us our debts, as we also have forgiven (left, remitted, and let go of the debts, and have given up resentment against) our debtors.

And lead (bring) us not into temptation, but deliver us from the evil one. *For Yours is the kingdom and the power and the glory forever. Amen.*

John 17:1-26 AMP

When Jesus had spoken these things, He lifted up His eyes to heaven and said, Father, the hour has come. Glorify and exalt and honor and magnify Your Son, so that Your Son may glorify and extol and honor and magnify You.

[Just as] You have granted Him power and authority over all flesh (all humankind), [now glorify Him] so that He may give eternal life to all whom You have given Him.

And this is eternal life: [it means] to know (to perceive, recognize, become acquainted with, and understand) You, the only true and real God, and [likewise] to know Him, Jesus [as the] Christ (the Anointed One, the Messiah), Whom You have sent.

I have glorified You down here on the earth by completing the work that You gave Me to do.

And now, Father, glorify Me along with Yourself and restore Me to such majesty and honor in Your presence as I had with You before the world existed.

I have manifested Your Name [I have revealed Your very Self, Your real Self] to the people whom You have given Me out of the world. They were Yours, and You gave them to Me, and they have obeyed and kept Your word.

Now [at last] they know and understand that all You have given Me belongs to You [is really and truly Yours].

For the [uttered] words that You gave Me I have given them; and they have received and accepted [them] and have come to know positively and in reality [to believe with absolute assurance] that I came forth from Your presence, and they have believed and are convinced that You did send Me.

I am praying for them. I am not praying (requesting) for the world, but for those You have given Me, for they belong to You.

All [things that are] Mine are Yours, and all [things that are] Yours belong to Me; and I am glorified in (through) them. [They have done Me honor; in them My glory is achieved.]

And [now] I am no more in the world, but these are [still] in the world, and I am coming to You. Holy Father, keep in Your Name [in the knowledge of Yourself] those whom You have given Me, that they may be one as We [are one].

While I was with them, I kept and preserved them in Your Name [in the knowledge and worship of You]. Those You have given Me I guarded and protected, and not one of them has perished or is lost except the son of perdition [Judas Iscariot—the one who is now doomed to destruction, destined to be lost], that the Scripture might be fulfilled. [Ps. 41:9; John 6:70.]

And now I am coming to You; I say these things while I am still in the world, so that My joy may be made full and complete and perfect in them [that they may experience My delight fulfilled in them, that My enjoyment may be perfected in their own souls, that they may have My gladness within them, filling their hearts].

I have given and delivered to them Your word (message) and the world has hated them, because they are not of the world [do not belong to the world], just as I am not of the world.

I do not ask that You will take them out of the world, but that You will keep and protect them from the evil one.

They are not of the world (worldly, belonging to the world), [just] as I am not of the world.

Sanctify them [purify, consecrate, separate them for Yourself, make them holy] by Truth; Your Word is Truth.

Just as You sent Me into the world, I also have sent them into the world.

And so for their sake and on their behalf I sanctify (dedicate, consecrate) Myself, that they also may be sanctified (dedicated, consecrated, made holy) in the Truth.

Neither for these alone do I pray [it is not for their sake only that I make this request], but also for all those who will ever come to believe in (trust in, cling to, rely on) Me through their word and teaching,

That they all may be one, [just] as You, Father, are in Me and I in You, that they also may be one in Us, so that the world may believe and be convinced that You have sent Me.

I have given to them the glory and honor which You have given Me, that they may be one [even] as We are one:

I in them and You in Me, in order that they may become one and perfectly united, that the world may know and [definitely] recognize that You sent Me and that You have loved them [even] as You have loved Me.

Father, I desire that they also whom You have entrusted to Me [as Your gift to Me] may be with Me where I am, so that they may see My glory, which You have given Me [Your love gift to Me]; for You loved Me before the foundation of the world.

O just and righteous Father, although the world has not known You and has failed to recognize You and has never acknowledged You, I have known you [continually]; and these men understand and know that You have sent Me.

I have made Your Name known to them and revealed Your character and Your very Self, and I will continue to make [You] known, that the love which You have bestowed upon Me may be in them [felt in their hearts] and that I [Myself] may be in them.

The Prayers of Paul

The Prayers of Paul

Ephesians 1:17-23 AMP

[For I always pray to] the God of our Lord Jesus Christ, the Father of glory, that He may grant you a spirit of wisdom and revelation [of insight into mysteries and secrets] in the [deep and intimate] knowledge of Him,

By having the eyes of your heart flooded with light, so that you can know and understand the hope to which He has called you, and how rich is His glorious inheritance in the saints (His set-apart ones),

And [so that you can know and understand] what is the immeasurable and unlimited and surpassing greatness of His power in and for us who believe, as demonstrated in the working of His mighty strength,

Which He exerted in Christ when He raised Him from the dead and seated Him at His [own] right hand in the heavenly [places],

Far above all rule and authority and power and dominion and every name that is named [above every title that can be conferred], not only in this age and in this world, but also in the age and the world which are to come.

And He has put all things under His feet and has appointed Him the universal and supreme Head of the church [a headship exercised throughout the church], [Ps. 8:6.]

Which is His body, the fullness of Him Who fills all in all [for in that body lives the full measure of Him Who makes everything complete, and Who fills everything everywhere with Himself].

Ephesians 3:14-21 AMP

For this reason [seeing the greatness of this plan by which you are built together in Christ], I bow my knees before the Father of our Lord Jesus Christ,

For Whom every family in heaven and on earth is named [that Father from Whom all fatherhood takes its title and derives its name].

May He grant you out of the rich treasury of His glory to be strengthened and reinforced with mighty power in the inner man by the [Holy] Spirit [Himself indwelling your innermost being and personality].

May Christ through your faith [actually] dwell (settle down, abide, make His permanent home) in your hearts! May you be rooted deep in love and founded securely on love,

That you may have the power and be strong to apprehend and grasp with all the saints [God's devoted people, the experience of that love] what is the breadth and length and height and depth [of it];

[That you may really come] to know [practically, through experience for yourselves] the love of Christ, which far surpasses mere knowledge [without experience]; that you may be filled [through all your being] unto all the fullness of God [may have the richest measure of the divine Presence, and become a body wholly filled and flooded with God Himself]!

Now to Him Who, by (in consequence of) the [action of His] power that is at work within us, is able to [carry out His purpose and] do superabundantly, far over and above all that we [dare] ask or think [infinitely beyond our highest prayers, desires, thoughts, hopes, or dreams] —

To Him be glory in the church and in Christ Jesus throughout all generations forever and ever. Amen (so be it).

Philippians 1:9-11 AMP

And this I pray: that your love may abound yet more and more and extend to its fullest development in knowledge and all keen insight [that your love may display itself in greater depth of acquaintance and more comprehensive discernment],

So that you may surely learn to sense what is vital, and approve and prize what is excellent and of real value [recognizing the highest and the best, and distinguishing the moral differences], and that you may be untainted and pure and unerring and blameless [so that with hearts sincere and certain and unsullied, you may approach] the day of Christ [not stumbling nor causing others to stumble].

May you abound in and be filled with the fruits of righteousness (of right standing with God and right doing) which come through Jesus Christ (the Anointed One), to the honor and praise of God [that His glory may be both manifested and recognized].

Colossians 1:9-12 AMP

For this reason we also, from the day we heard of it, have not ceased to pray and make [special] request for you, [asking] that you may be filled with the full (deep and clear) knowledge of His will in all spiritual wisdom [in comprehensive insight into the ways and purposes of God] and in understanding and discernment of spiritual things —

That you may walk (live and conduct yourselves) in a manner worthy of the Lord, fully pleasing to Him and desiring to please Him in all things, bearing fruit in every good work and steadily growing and increasing in and by the knowledge of God [with fuller, deeper, and clearer insight, acquaintance, and recognition].

[We pray] that you may be invigorated and strengthened with all power according to the might of His glory, [to exercise] every kind of endurance and patience (perseverance and forbearance) with joy,

Giving thanks to the Father, Who has qualified and made us fit to share the portion which is the inheritance of the saints (God's holy people) in the Light.

2 Thessalonians 1:11,12 AMP

With this in view we constantly pray for you, that our God may deem and count you worthy of [your] calling and [His] every gracious purpose of goodness, and with power may complete in [your] every particular work of faith (faith which is that leaning of the whole human personality on God in absolute trust and confidence in His power, wisdom, and goodness).

Thus may the name of our Lord Jesus Christ be glorified and become more glorious through and in you, and may you [also be glorified] in Him according to the grace (favor and blessing) of our God and the Lord Jesus Christ (the Messiah, the Anointed One).

MISSION STATEMENT

Word Ministries, Inc.

To motivate individuals to spiritual growth and emotional wholeness, encouraging them to become more deeply and intimately acquainted with the Father God as they pray *Prayers That Avail Much*.

Other Books by Word Ministries, Inc.

Prayers That Avail Much—Volume 2

Prayers That Avail Much—Volume 3

Oraciones Con Poder
Prayers That Avail Much
Spanish edition

Prayers That Avail Much for Business Professionals

Prayers That Avail Much—Special Edition
leather

Prayers That Avail Much for Mothers
pocket size

Prayers That Avail Much for Mothers
leather

Prayers That Avail Much Commemorative Gift Edition

Prayers That Avail Much for Fathers

Prayers That Avail Much for Women

Prayers That Avail Much for Teens
revised pocket edition

Prayers That Avail Much for Kids

Prayers That Avail Much Daily Calendar

Available from your local bookstore.

Harrison House
Tulsa, OK 74153

About the Author

Germaine Griffin Copeland, founder and president of Word Ministries, Inc., is the author of the *Prayers That Avail Much* family of books. Her writings provide scriptural prayer instruction to help you pray effectively for those things that concern you and your family and for other prayer assignments. Her teachings on prayer, the personal growth of the intercessor, emotional healing and related subjects have brought understanding, hope, healing and liberty to the discouraged and emotionally wounded. She is a woman of prayer and praise whose highest form of worship is the study of God's Word. Her greatest desire is to know God.

Word Ministries, Inc., is a prayer and teaching ministry. Germaine believes that God has called her to teach the practical application of the Word of Truth for successful, victorious living. After years of searching diligently for truth and trying again and again to come out of depression, she decided that she was a mistake. Out of the depths of despair she called upon the name of the Lord, and the light of God's presence invaded the room where she was sitting.

It was in that moment that she experienced the warmth of God's love; old things passed away, and she felt brand new. She discovered a motivation for living—life had purpose. Living in the presence of God, she has found unconditional love and acceptance, healing for crippled emotions, contentment that overcomes depression, peace in the midst of adverse circumstances, and grace for developing healthy relationships. The ongoing process of transformation evolved into praying for others, and the prayer of intercession became her prayer focus.

Germaine is the daughter of Reverend A. H. "Buck" Griffin and the late Donnis Brock Griffin. She and her husband, Everette, have four children, five grandchildren and two great-grandchildren. Germaine and Everette reside in Sandy Springs, a suburb of Atlanta, Georgia.

You may contact
Word Ministries
by writing:

Word Ministries, Inc.
38 Sloan Street
Roswell, Georgia 30075
or calling 770-518-1065
www.prayers.org

*Please include your prayer requests
and comments when you write.*

The Harrison House Vision

Proclaiming the truth and the power

Of the Gospel of Jesus Christ

With excellence;

Challenging Christians to

Live victoriously,

Grow spiritually,

Know God intimately.